Poetry's Old Air

POETS ON POETRY · Donald Hall, General Editor

Marianne Boruch

Poetry's Old Air

Ann Arbor

THE UNIVERSITY OF MICHIGAN PRESS

Copyright © by the University of Michigan 1995
All rights reserved
Published in the United States of America by
The University of Michigan Press
Manufactured in the United States of America

1998   1997   1996   1995   4   3   2   1

A CIP catalogue record for this book is available from the British Library.

Library of Congress Cataloging-in-Publication Data

Boruch, Marianne, 1950–
    Poetry's old air / Marianne Boruch.
        p.   cm. — (Poets on poetry)
    Includes bibliographical references (p.   ) and index.
    ISBN 0-472-09584-6 (acid-free paper).—ISBN 0-472-06584-X
(pbk. : acid-free paper)
    1. Boruch, Marianne, 1950–   —Aesthetics.   2. American
poetry—20th century—History and criticism.   3. Poetics.
I. Title.   II. Series.
PS3552.07564564   1995
811.009—dc20   94-44312
                                                      CIP

In memory of Leonora Woodman,
continual spirit

Acknowledgments

I want to thank the editors of the following publications for first printing these essays, all of which have been changed somewhat for this collection. The first four pieces listed here came about by invitation, and to those editors—Michael Martone, Stephen Corey and Stan Lindbergh, David Hamilton—I am especially grateful: *Townships*, University of Iowa Press, 1992, "The Quiet House"; the *Georgia Review* "Dickinson Descending" and "Hopkins by Heart"; the *Iowa Review* "Thirst and Patience" and "Poetry's Old Air"; the *Massachusetts Review* "Poetry and Its Rubble"; *Parnassus* "Plath's Bees"; the *Southern Review* "The Sound of It"; the *Ohio Review* "On Metaphor." I also wish to thank the Georgia Poetry Circuit whose invitation prompted the essay "Poetry and Its Rubble."

Sections in "Plath's Bees" from Plath's unpublished drafts are quoted here by permission, as are the lines from Moore's sketchbooks in "Thirst and Patience." My thanks again to Olwyn Hughes, literary executor of the estate of Sylvia Plath, and to Clive Driver, literary executor of the estate of Marianne Moore at the time I wrote the essay. My reference in "On Metaphor" to Jamie Chrisman's unpublished work is also here by permission.

Finally, I am grateful to Purdue University's School of Liberal Arts for the grant that gave me the time to write "Hopkins by Heart."

Contents

Introduction

The essay is a curious form, closer in its meditative possibilities to poetry than is usually imagined. So it seems natural to work toward it as one might work toward a poem, with reverence for mystery and accident. Still, I had reason; I wanted to write these pieces to understand the work of others, giving myself plenty of time to stare and to figure. I think now that I wanted to define poetry for myself, or at least approach a definition. *I worked from memory and example*—the phrase is Louise Bogan's. And both impulses lie behind this collection, the wish to draw on personal experience as well as from living example. But these impulses are not equal. The latter is greater here, and my choices—Frost, Dickinson, Plath, Hopkins, Bishop, among others—have been guided by gratitude for certain poems that mean and continue to mean. I've tried, in whatever wayward way I could manage, to pay attention, and to honor such work. No agenda but that.

But there are those who influenced how I approached these essays. Six of the pieces were given as lectures at the MFA program at Warren Wilson College, and I owe much to students and colleagues there for their spirited support. My students in the English Department at Purdue, and my colleagues there, particularly Margaret Moan Rowe, Neil Myers, and Bill Stuckey, matter more than they know. Other Purdue colleagues were generous to me, and crucial to the making of two of these essays—William J. Fischang, of Entomology, who showed me the University's hives, and Paul Dubowey, of Forestry, who allowed me to audit his ornithology class. Good friends Brigit Kelly and Joy Manesiotis gave me invaluable advice, especially in the final stages as I put this thing together. And for two, there will never be enough thanks—David Dunlap, steadfast listener, patient and articulate critic who believed from the start. And Will Dunlap, for his cheerful interest, always asking—from the age of three on up—how whatever essay it was, was going.

Poetry's Old Air

This past year I bought a bicycle at a yard sale where every-thing was going: the kids' beds from long ago, the refrigerator right out of the kitchen, years of clothing, not old enough to be valuable, just embarrassing, said the woman in charge, laughing as she bagged the skirts with too many pleats, the ties too wide. My bicycle, however, was perfect: balloon tires, coaster brakes, the sensible upright seat. Blue. Of course, it was a woman's—or as one says, a girl's bike—with its center bar at a slope, for skirts, or at least for gentle stops. I walked the thing home. The tires, though filled, weren't quite as firm as I liked; I didn't want to risk their damage. I figured they'd be hard to replace in this era of skinny cool-guy wheels.

Once home, I fell into the old habit of my other bike, the one with the baby seat still on back, with its hand brakes that don't work, the one whose gears have dwindled down to the hardest one, making me a pioneer to ride it: great god, horri-ble snow, if we can just hold out another minute, or hour, three weeks until spring, and so on. Old stupid habits, per-haps, but before long, that bike had a flat, and I was fiddling hard to get the air pump on my "new" bike, the blue one.

I was in a rush, which is the root of all evil and most sur-prise, and I bent to the little cap still on the tube's air nozzle. The woman who sold the bike had said no one had touched it for years, its tires last inflated, she was sure, in 1962, when her daughter turned eighteen, bought the Chevy, and ditched the bike for good. So I was turning the little cap, hurrying to fit the air pump to it. Soon I would be late for class, my students both pleased and disgruntled by my absence.

But it was the old air that got me, shooting out when I

pressed the pump to the nozzle, old air, sweet and vile at once, in there some twenty-eight years. Air, I suddenly realized, from 1962, pre-Reagan, pre-Nixon air, Kennedy-still-alive air, the world still *postwar*, sex still *premarital*, everything stalled at a slant, either foreshadowing or looking back. I was twelve— was I ever really twelve?—and grandparents were a given. This old air, then, on this old street, two blocks from the river: it could do the impossible; it could transform.

❦

I think of this moment, carry it around, perhaps to solve something. But if poetry is more than the "click" of its revelation, if it is, as well, a process, an invited, even willed habit, then I need to go elsewhere, jump time and place, not simply months but too many years to Amherst, Massachusetts, where I was trying to make pots, a matter far removed from that moment where a bike might astonish like a genie sprung from a lamp. It was, instead, months of long afternoons and dusty wheels, of scary, nasty glazes—every one of them poisonous— and the rowdy camaraderie of the studio, all, on the face of it, a great relief from poetry, a kind of inverse world Alice found down her rabbit hole, the sort Russell Edson unearths by a design of peculiar brilliance. I was at UMass then, in the writing program, making my slow way toward a graduate degree. I'd walk over afternoons, shrugging off workshops and literature, and disappear among the earnest, madcap potters. I never was really one of them. A year and a half later, I was still deftly turning would-be Grecian urns into dog dishes. *Time on the wheel,* my teacher, Susan Parks, kept telling us when we whined and cursed. Each disaster gets you closer to the bowl, the cup, the pitcher that will be *enough*, which is to say, simply itself. I think I was addicted; that trance over the turning wheel, that opening up each mound of clay smoothly, the earth of it, the water. And I recall particularly one morning, a Saturday in the large airy upstairs room, spring, the windows open to the new air, Beethoven's *Pastorale* on WFCR coming off someone's mud-splashed radio. Just a few of us working that early. Just a few. And we were at it intently, in silence.

All that patience, that play between intention and empti-
ness might have been the real gift: a fist full of clay turned
into something again and again. It had everything to do with
poems. One becomes a writer, in time. In time, one becomes a
writer. Then more time passes, and one becomes a writer. So
the growth of the imagination takes forever, a lifetime anyway.
But I'm probably digressing. In that room then, in that
trance above the wheel, I found the pleasure of the making
itself: it took me out of time. It wasn't just the historical jolt, the
potter's wheel, though that was happily confusing as well—
easily 1850 or 100 B.C. any place on the planet, the ancients
turning out their dog dishes too. It went further than "the
past," further out of time. For I don't think poets or any artists,
really, are *in time* at all. The poem, the process of making a
poem, is our stay against time, perhaps against history, against
what is public and broadly—often emptily—communal and
handed to us, against speech even, for all the words in a poem
both emerge from, and finally add up to silence, whatever
beauty and terror that may mean.

The terror is not simply in the result—those images we
manage to call up—but in the process itself. I'm haunted, for
instance, by a prose poem of Gregory Orr's, his "Hotel St.
Louis, New York City, Fall 1969," an account of the young
man he was, just a kid really, at a crummy evening job, his
deluxe piss-in-the-sink room at a wino hotel—this, against the
morning's real work, the disappearance into "drafts of poems,
dream journals, stray ideas." But this stays with me: one
week's grueling exercise in memory—a daily twenty minutes
all he could stand—closing his eyes to open the house of his
childhood, entering there to see things, pausing methodically
over the hooked rug, the cane seat, a whole wall where find-
ing nothing day after day, he winced and turned away. More
details seen and cherished until, he writes, "my head started
to buzz and I had to stop." Until "late that week I woke up
knowing I'd lost control of my mind. . . ."

The striking thing about this exercise is that it appears at
first so ordinary, not particularly dramatic at all. Simple things
are evoked—the latticed porch, a gray and white Chevy
parked under a weeping birch outside. Just details, but they

carry one elsewhere and buoy up memory until—what?—
even the weight of these small, idle things is too much. They
begin to have a life of their own. They begin to *mean*.

Intention and emptiness, that patience—over the potter's
wheel or before the blank page—is trance, and crucial, I sup-
pose, to all art, but especially to poetry. We deal day and night
in memory, not nostalgia, the value of which is discovery, not
sentiment, and one empties to find it. Memories persist and
are personal. But if tapped for their strangeness, they often
begin to assume weight, historical or mythic, even a spiritual
weight, as if these poor shards we find in our lives were really
part of a larger buried vessel.

One last thought on this. A man in my department at Pur-
due, Bill Bache, a veteran of the Second World War, tells a
true story to his Shakespeare students. It's a clandestine story
of war and rescue, he and three others taken prisoner on a
country road near Innsbruck, 1945, by several other young
men who could've easily been their German doubles. The
man remembers himself wounded in the attack and brought
out of a thicket, lying there in the sun. His friends are led off
and he is left with three of his captors, boys really. He under-
stands that these young men are deciding whether to kill him
or not, though no one says a word. They come closer and he
fumbles in his jacket for a pack of cigarettes—partially soaked
with his own blood—and holds it out to the oldest one. The
boy shrugs, and reaches, each one now carefully drawing out
a cigarette, leaning back, smoking, talking. A reprieve that is
working. It will be the end of the war in about ten minutes.
American troops are marching that moment. Soon they will
be visible, turning toward them as the road itself turns.

My students—our students—so much younger than either
of us, play this over in their heads. It falls on them like sudden
light or rain, briefly unthinkable, the stuff of myth, this rescue
in the nick of time and no, not a movie at all. They are touched
by it, certainly touched by their passionate teacher stopping to
tell it against *Hamlet* and *King Lear*, giving them a lens and a
focus. I love the story, love its lit secret presence in this seem-
ingly ordinary man walking down our low-ceilinged hallway,
his drive to give it away in the middle of Shakespeare, himself a

genius of gory scenes and terrible coincidences. I can't get that hand out of my mind—its desperate, sweet gesture, that bloody pack of cigarettes, the sunny day, the Germans, so young and uncertain. Borges in his small parable, "The Witness," mourns the death of the last worshiper of Woden, the last to see those pagan rites, though he ends in a startling personal shift. "What will die with me when I die," he writes, "what pathetic or fragile form will the world lose? The voice of Macedonio Fernandez, the image of a red horse in a vacant lot at Serrano and Charcas, a bar of sulphur in a drawer of a mahogany desk?"

❦

It's a curious matter. We believe in time, our days are passed as *days*, capsuled out neatly into human-made "work weeks" but kept by natural cycle too—autumn's daft dismemberment, spring's foolish resurrection on cue. Yet going back through memory to more memory, we both honor and dismiss such measurement of things. I said poets work outside of, even against time; I mean we put ourselves in the precarious moment, taking on the trance that brings up poems, to see, perhaps, as the future sees if its crystal ball looked back. Not that we would be left there in that childhood house or on that German country road, but that we can't be. And so the enormous longing, the dark *duende* that Lorca speaks of, that sense of death, its presence, enters all great poems.

By poetry, I mean both lyric and narrative, trusting their sister/brotherhood against the current argument that would divide them into little warring kingdoms, a division that would have us finally confess (confess!) and choose: is it the self or the world that absorbs us?—as if the best poems didn't work their power at the point where these two visions, public and private, collapse into each other. Elizabeth Bishop's poem, "In the Waiting Room," which itself is born of memory, is an astonishing example of this frightening, necessary merging, but that's not the piece that concerns me here.

"Poem," which appeared in *Geography III*, her last book, is—and as a lyric of rich, interior order it automatically faces all the dangers of that form: self-aggrandizement, an easy appropriation of another's pain, an intensity whipped up to a cartoon of itself ("So much depends on *me* glazed with rain beside the white chickens"). It risks the reverse too, the problem of the prosaic, narrative's obsession with detail, too much world—chickens or rain or glazed wheelbarrows—with no real way into it through the poet's handmade lens. Now that I've reduced this argument to its minuscule theory—yet another cartoon—we can dismiss it, as Bishop seems to, for what she manages in "Poem" seems to me somehow distant from either the self "in here" or the world "out there." Instead, we move along in that scary fluid of mind—*thinking*, the process connecting these two visions, and what "Poem" is really about, Bishop's meandering trance to bring together her experience and her uncle's, set apart by decades. "About the size of an old-style dollar," she begins,

> American or Canadian,
> mostly the same whites, gray greens, and steel grays
> —this little painting (a sketch for a larger one?)
> has never earned any money in its life.
> Useless and free, it has spent seventy years
> as a minor family relic
> handed along collaterally to owners
> who looked at it sometimes, or didn't bother to.
>
> It must be Nova Scotia; only there
> does one see gabled wooden houses
> painted that awful shade of brown.
> The other houses, the bits that show, are white.
> Elm trees, low hills, a thin church steeple
> —that gray-blue wisp—or is it? In the foreground
> a water meadow with some tiny cows,
> two brushstrokes each, but confidently cows;
> two minuscule white geese in the blue water,
> back-to-back, feeding, and a slanting stick.
> Up closer, a wild iris, white and yellow,
> fresh-squiggled from the tube.
> The air is fresh and cold; cold early spring
> clear as gray glass; a half inch of blue sky
> below steel-gray storm clouds.

(They were the artist's specialty.)
A specklike bird is flying to the left.
Or is it a flyspeck looking like a bird?

Heavens, I recognize the place, I know it!
It's behind—I can almost remember the farmer's name.
His barn backed on that meadow. There it is,
titanium white, one dab. The hint of steeple,
filaments of brush-hairs, barely there,
must be the Presbyterian church.
Would that be Miss Gillespie's house?
Those particular geese and cows
are naturally before my time.

A sketch done in an hour, "in one breath,"
once taken from a trunk and handed over.
Would you like this? I'll probably never
have room to hang these things again.
Your Uncle George, no, mine, my Uncle George,
he'd be your great-uncle, left them all with Mother
when he went back to England.
You know, he was quite famous, an R.A. . . .

I never knew him. We both knew this place,
apparently, this literal small backwater,
looked at it long enough to memorize it,
our years apart. How strange. And it's still loved,
or its memory is (it must have changed a lot).
Our visions coincided—"visions" is
too serious a word—our looks, two looks:
art "copying from life" and life itself,
life and the memory of it so compressed
they've turned into each other. Which is which?
Life and the memory of it cramped,
dim, on a piece of Bristol board,
dim, but how live, how touching in detail
—the little that we get for free,
the little of our earthly trust. Not much.
About the size of our abidance
along with theirs: the munching cows,
the iris, crisp and shivering, the water
still standing from spring freshets,
the yet-to-be dismantled elms, the geese.

Bishop's method is fragmentary, deep with suggestion; one thing reminds her of another as we move back through time. Her literal subject—one of her favorites—is homemade art, however accomplished, art not heightened by brilliant technique but kept personal and surprising by the exactitude of its maker, here an artist with a "specialty" ("steel-gray storm clouds"), her great-uncle George, long passed to more exotic regions. The painting, "useless and free" and a "minor family relic," is a window to George's time; it is George's eye, as quirky—this must be genetic—as Bishop's, this uncle who could keep a wild iris going "fresh-squiggled from the tube" or bring a barn to life with "titanium white, one dab" or the church, clearly Presbyterian by the steeple's "filaments of brush-hairs, barely there." One looks playfully and hard at all this, exactly as the niece is looking, right now. Her present tense carries this power to animate, but the odd turns in the lines—questions, afterthoughts, exclamations, asides in their fussy, edgy press—all mime the agile mind thinking, and in the process, the blur of George's hand at the canvas—*his* "fresh-squiggling" after all, *his* dabbing, *his* dubious choice of "that awful shade of brown." The niece is merely our able translator. *Merely.*

This is sometimes Bishop's role for herself, especially early in poems, a kind of "as told to" stance, even when she is telling herself these things, thinking out loud, trying things out in a loud stage whisper. This modesty is part of her work's lucid power: one never doubts she is waylaying pretense because though her instinct is spontaneous, she does not presume. Amid this care for boundaries, the remarkable thing is how time and its borders dissolve in the poem anyway. George's picture works as abstractly as some looming contraption out of science fiction regardless of Bishop's concern to keep it hard and fast with painterly detail. We fall easily through it, not only to witness the poet's own discovery, then George himself—his brushwork as immediate gesture—but finally full flight into the landscape itself, a place so cast in movement through Bishop's reverie that it's alive, returned to this moment of "feeding" geese and flying "specklike" birds. It's childhood, recalled by places complete with names, Miss Gillespie's house, for instance, unaltered, as if nothing really changes things, certainly not death. By now George has done his job and essentially disappeared. The time is Bishop's—"Heavens, I recognize the place, I know it!"—a moment of personal focus, half certitude, half longing, close to the stunning shift she so admired as a college student, reading Hopkins—she told Ashley Brown in interview—and finding in "The Wreck of the Deutschland", in that poem's tedium, a sudden flare into imaginative energy. "Fancy, come faster" Hopkins cried out in the middle of things, speaking, as Bishop does, directly, his passion compelling because, like hers, it seems so private. We have simply overheard.

This "overheard" quality, as Auden called it, has been in ✓ lyric verse from the beginning, recent evidence coming through Yeats' definition, so famous it is nearly cliché—"one's argument with oneself"—that works poetry against its gregarious sibling, rhetoric, where one's argument remains "with the ✓ world." But Bishop's method is memory, that place of such interior depth and surprise that the leap of time dissolves even argument. "Our visions coincided—" she says of herself and her uncle, though adding quickly, with characteristic humility, "'visions' is / too serious a word—our looks, two looks: / . . . Life and the memory of it cramped, / dim, on a piece of Bristol board, / dim, but how live, how touching in detail / —the little that we get for free, / the little of our earthly trust. Not much." But how one cherishes this little we do get—the "shivering" iris, the heartbreaking "yet-to-be-dismantled elms," the wayward geese—things seen sideways as if Bishop were speaking fitfully again, to herself. One is smitten by it, but not in the way ✓ the flash of epiphany in a more conventional lyric poem might come, or the way story haunts in more narrative verse. Not, not in the same way at all.

Talking with a friend, a poet, Tam Lin Neville, I sense a nagging distrust of classic forms come back, she wanting poems to be more faithful to the real rhythm of our days, the way things drift, the small offhand gifts. As if life were like that, she says of the lyric, one revelation after another. Or narrative, I ✓ say, as if everything works out in a curve so neatly. Perhaps it's just that we hunger for a sense of time both larger and more ordinary than that, more plural. It is a mystery how things go and return and go, a mystery that belongs to poetry, and, oddly, though we value great turns and desperate moments—all the bloody cigarettes of the lyric, those moments that give even narrative verse its flight and release, its *poetry*—it needn't always be so dramatic. Bishop is not dramatic; she is possible. I think of those elms until I can no longer think.

❦

We are back to image, I suppose, and its power, the power of the partial, the unfinished that is human. It is a dailiness our mortality allows: one is able to pin down that much. Meanwhile, other poets have been keeping track, George Oppen, say, writing for no one in his daybook, private notes he kept for years. "Love of the world: it is not merely a sunny day in the country: it is the love of fate." Or this: "It is necessary to study the words you have written for the words have a longer history than you have and say more than you know." Or this: "On writing a poem; not to make noise: to keep one's attention outward toward silence."

All through May, I am reading such things, or avoiding reading such things by disappearing outside, working spring into the garden, making new borders in the hopeless shade. A place in Minnesota sends me special plants for shade—balloon flower and anthemis and the slow hulking monkshood. But they don't send me what I expect, stems and leaves, only roots, strange squid-like twisted shapes I hardly know how to plant, all huge and terrible and quite unlike each other in their little plastic bags. I take them out, and hold them in my hand. I can almost hear their ticking, the wise dumb clockwork within that will send up straight stems, astonishing color, this ugly silent buried thing propelling so lush a fate.

But sometimes fate seems the buried thing alone. There's a great world far from my tiny American orbit of yard and house and town. And all through May this year in Beijing's Tiananmen Square, thousands are assembling while the army makes its reluctant though hardening way toward them. I think again of the "shivering iris," the "yet-to-be dismantled elms." How these things, singular, merely themselves, are able to absorb such darkness, quietly, to *become* dramatic, expanding to encompass whole movements of history and neglect and violence. It's been years now, of course, since Bishop wrote, but her images against the thick swirl of recent events focus and still them for me even as the iris and the elm remain strictly and mysteriously *not* anywhere but here, in Bishop's poem, in her intelligent and specific composure of memory. Oppen's right—not a sunny day in the country, this love of the world, but a love of fate. As for the fate of a poem, who can tell what that will be, as if we knew even a fraction of its cost, or its treasure.

Are there poems really left to write? I have heard students, beginning poets, ask in equal parts grief and gratitude for the rich layers of poem we've built up by the thousands over centuries. Hasn't everything already been written? I find myself saying, yes, everything. Everything but the poems your generation, or any living generation for that matter, will write from its particular experience. Being twenty-three now is, after all, worlds apart from being twenty-three in 1973 or 1952 or 1929, and in time one begins to see how. At that moment, even poems of immense privacy, lyric or narrative, begin to bear a different weight, a release, however peripherally, into historical meaning that accounts, accounts *for*.

But one cannot worry this edge into things; the threat of rhetoric is too close. Our power remains in the *lived* thing, or as Oppen in his poem, "Of Being Numerous," says, in "the isolation of the actual," where one talks "of rooms, and of what they look out on and of basements, the rough wall bearing the marks of the forms . . . such solitude as we know—." Our eye remains on the image as it makes its immediate leaps and deliberations, as it moves to create shape, the story, however fitful. It should and does surprise us how that movement, through the mind's swift, slow-angled lens, suggests something larger than our little dumbstruck time and place.

In Oppen's poem, "Niece," that lens makes things riveting because, like Bishop, Oppen keeps himself in the delicate

place of mind exactly between what is public and private, and
so becomes heir to both.

> The streets of San Francisco,
> She said of herself, were my
>
> Father and mother, speaking to the quiet guests
> In the living room looking down the hills
>
> To the bay. And we imagined her
> Walking in the wooded past
> Of the western city . . . her mother
>
> Was not that city
> But my eldest sister. I remembered
>
> The watchman at the beach
> Telling us the war had ended—
>
> That was the first world war
> Half a century ago—my sister
> Had a ribbon in her hair.

The poem, at first, seems to begin elsewhere, out of the
speaker's control with the niece bragging lightly and bitterly
of raising herself, the streets her real parents, all this in front
of the "quiet guests" who appear to have nothing at stake.
Outside is the bay—blue water one invents quickly, the hills
dropping to it, though this young woman is our focus, burn-
ing up the mild living room with her sad bravado. In neither
defense nor condemnation, the poet, the uncle here though
brother still to the woman disdained, claims his sister through
sudden memory, fifty years ago, where a "watchman at the
beach" tells them that "the war had ended— . . . my sister"
Oppen adds, "had a ribbon in her hair."

In that image, that ribbon, we needle down through five
decades of family history, but how poignantly the poem opens
further to the larger historical moment, closing not just with
sister or brother, but the watchman too, these three looking
out at the endless water, dazed, probably, at the massive
news—the world war ended, the first of this century. That this
child with her careful, vibrant ribbon is buried in the mother
of this other child so grown-up and furious who stalks the

present room, is a source not of particular pain but of wonder. I think of Czeslaw Milosz recalling in his poem, "Encounter," an ordinary wagon and bird, a friend's hand pointing to the flash of wing overhead a lifetime ago, and his asking "not out of sorrow but in wonder" what happens that these things are vanished.

It strikes me that poetry—all art perhaps—carries within itself two mysteries, each with its own sense of time. If I'm right about *trance*, if time is stopped to begin the poem, then perversely, a conventional, human measurement is echoed and mimed to keep the poor thing going. This might be the art of it, those intricate interior wheels and pulleys with their real world pretense—the hand midair and birds that feed or fly, a watchman so full of news he'd talk even to children, a foreboding habit—a specialty—in steel-gray storm clouds, all the compression of *story* cut to the bare miraculous, the image and its suggestive cubist shards. These things move us through time; they mime the growth and diminishment of things, and so imply the mortality of earth and the body, the lure of the dramatic that is so difficult to resist. We hear it too, in the cadence that settles and rises in the wheeling, snaking, bursting sentence made breathless and strange by the poetic line. So we measure time, and in that act suggest what is public and communal, what is, in fact, history. In spite of ourselves and against the stopped, still origin of our impulse, we remake time in some odd homemade way, moving along until that too vanishes.

Those years ago I remember my pottery teacher stood over our bowls and jars at critiques, tracing their turns, holding them up eye level, centering their weight in both hands. Form is finally about what's not in a piece, she told us once, twice, too many times to count. Don't crowd the emptiness out of it, she said.

❦

Charles Simic's poems have always seemed to me to bear such weight, this shadow—really a kind of closure—from their initial lines, as if vanishing were the norm, the spirit's cottage industry. "On the first page of my dreambook / It's always evening / In an occupied country," he begins in his poem, "Empire of Dreams." And we believe him the way we believe the old widower down the block who refuses to throw out his wife's dresses. That continual pull of silence and darkness elevates, makes each image, for the moment at least, saved, and for that rescue joyful, no matter how melancholy the news might be. And public or private, lyric or narrative, these dark elements seem so intertwined that the poems enter, as if sleepwalking, a place beyond the historical into what is mythic.

His poem "Prodigy" lives in all regions. "I grew up bent over a chessboard," Simic tells us first.

> I loved the word endgame.
>
> All my cousins looked worried.
>
> It was a small house
> near a Roman graveyard.
>
> Planes and tanks
> shook the windowpanes.
>
> A retired professor of astronomy
> taught me how to play.
>
> That must have been in 1944.
>
> In the set we were using,
> the paint had almost chipped off
> the black pieces.
>
> The white King was missing
> and had to be substituted for.
>
> I'm told but do not believe
> that that summer I witnessed
> men hung from telephone poles.
>
> I remember my mother
> blindfolding me a lot.
>
> She had a way of tucking my head
> suddenly under her overcoat.

In chess, too, the professor told me,
the masters play blindfolded,
the great ones on several boards
at the same time.

At once we are in the most interior and exterior circumstance, drawn first through a personal memory of wartime, the speaker's boyhood love of chess against that violent other world where he witnessed—though he refuses to remember—"men hung from telephone poles." Outside then this matter-of-fact cruelty, while inside, the reverse: the old astronomy professor teaching the boy chess, this boy who, nevertheless, loves the word "endgame" as much as the ruined particulars—the set itself whose paint "had almost chipped off," the white king that "is missing." One passes weeks and months through the game's gentle mimicking of war, in this "small house / near a Roman graveyard," a fact that roots us centuries. But it is the mother's instinct to keep the boy blind to the outside horrors—"she had this way of tucking my head, suddenly under her overcoat"—that alters what enormous ground is already covered, taking things further, releasing us from past or present fact into a future made possible only by such innocence. "In chess, too, the professor told me," Simic writes in closing, "the masters play blindfolded, the great ones on several boards at the same time."

It occurs to me that this poem works as myth does; it presses itself into the future by the play of innocence and knowledge, pitting the great composure within the house against the unthinkable disorder outside, the boy as the blind still eye at the center. It is repeatable, allegorical pattern, the mother's foreboding, love in her impulse to keep tragedy hidden. Her gesture—turning the boy so he cannot see—has ceremonial grace; we jump whole eras by it and in the final image of the blind masters at their simultaneous boards, the entire business turns nearly Olympian, those in control high and oblivious, unseeing in their power. Who are they, languid over their games, consumed with tricks and detail? What do they know of happiness or sorrow? Such an ending does something else: it does not end. Instead, it keeps the poem from vanishing, or more accurately, through it, the poem vanishes into something more haunting than our human-made machinery can figure, past the lie that we understand things—ourselves among them—or that our understanding is complete.

As for the poet, such movement keeps ambition as it should be: enormous and modest, both. "The great gesture," Simic said in an interview with Barry Lopez in 1972, "the selfless poetic act is timeless, a moment outside history. . . . In some curious way," he added, "that gesture is anonymous . . . greater than our destiny. . . . We make the gesture, then, in the name of everyone who has ever lived."

❦

Still, however poignant the force of that gesture, we eventually find a way out of the poem, drift out of that trance, though it's not so easy. Whole critical careers, of course, have been built on the outside of this issue—"poetic closure"—articles, books, entire conferences orbiting this term and its portentous final ring. But if you think as I do that longing makes the poem in the first place, longing built somehow into image and language, the whole design pitched at that forward angle, then that term—poetic closure—is largely fake, an oxymoron. There is, after all, that final glimpse before the door clicks shut—light still falling through the ancient, thinning elms, a boy whistling home from a summer job, a black dog paused by the fence across the street: treasures, however off-hand, continuing, which is to say, *possible*, beyond our poor definition or invention.

If Lorca in his way was right, if poems concern what vanishes, then mysteriously, that's what stays. The last word quits and we have this lovely vacuum. We're there, staring down the hole, the poem's echo still in our heads, its afterimage still on everything, the afternoon changed seriously by the blunt strange air released by whatever orphaned bicycle. My point is this: the poem keeps going, off to where no instrument can count it, off *out of time*, which is to say, past the body and beyond even memory, where the trance began. Perhaps it is like that moment when we were little and aimed our flashlights at the stars on summer nights. Someone, the smart kid—Mickey Ingolia on my block—always said that our lights kept going. In a million years, two million, they might reach some bright pinpoint in the Big Dipper or in Cassiopeia. And so we stood there, beaming up loop-de-loops, clicking our flashlights off and on, all of us struck suddenly with such hopelessness and purpose.

Dickinson Descending

So many begin, not with her, but with her house. It is a pecu-
liarly American instinct, for all our restlessness, this passion
for place: to be there, to see—as far as a century allows—as
she saw, which is to say, *what* she saw. In Adrienne Rich's
struggles with Emily Dickinson, we are talked right into the
room where she wrote and slept; Rich calls herself "an insect,
vibrating at the frames of the window," offers us the bed, the
small desk with its single drawer, the view that launches us,
but secretly, into the Amherst street, Main Street, below. *Enclo-
sure.* To be enclosed as we imagine Dickinson was, as we have
been told over and over into somnambulant litany she was.
For men, as for women, this pilgrimage is true, though Allen
Ginsberg—I heard this once, did it really happen?—skipped
the famous bedroom in his rush for the attic, as if genius like
heat could rise and linger. He wished only to sit and say noth-
ing in that air, to meditate the afternoon. Returning to the
women who kept the house shiny and sealed as tableau, he
told them—jubilantly, matter-of-factly, who knows?—he had
levitated there, right above them in the attic. Put a camera on
those women watching that luminous, scraggly man, son of
Whitman in our lifetime; watch them waver quietly between
amusement and belief. "All men say 'what' to me," Dickinson
wrote the *Atlantic Monthly* editor Thomas Higginson when she
was thirty-two, "but I thought it a fashion"—a fashion we
stubbornly continue with curiosity, with bewilderment and rel-
ish, past the gentility of those New Critics or deconstruc-
tionists who would discreetly part the human life from poems.
Homage: every visit, and years of studies on Dickinson, and

so much of it personal yet remarkably inventive, like the fisherman who praises the trout with his glittering hooked flies. More, the need is almost physical not unlike the passion of Rodin tracking down Balzac, dead some thirty years, by spending weeks in Balzac's Tours preparing for the famous sculpture, drawing every old man in sight, rereading the novels, even finding Balzac's aging tailor and shaking from him the writer's measurements and preferences for fabric and style. Then the new dressing gown, new waistcoat, and trousers Rodin ordered, and his hanging them, a kind of reverse human scaffolding, in his Paris studio—memory lured out with weave and substance, hard facts for the sculptor, not dream.

There's the common intelligence on Dickinson, old as old teeth: the white dress; the willingness to talk, but only behind doors left minutely ajar; the freckles; the flowers, heliotrope and lady's slipper; and the small whimsies, deliberate as windows through which, unseen, she dropped down strings of candy to children waiting gleefully below. So many books relive her life, her brother's and sister's lives, her father's life; articles continue her garden, her breads and puddings, her eye troubles, her greenhouse. This cottage industry veers and grows into whole villages and towns—even cities, probably complete with mayors and aldermen—or into remoter places where one imagines the pleased selectman handing out the silken ribbons over bouquets of unearthed fact. Even popular culture fumes and bubbles the mystery: Julie Harris in her Dickinson road show, on stage and record, takes the poet past herself into parody—kittenish and coy and allowed, as women sometimes are, a brief but glorious rebellion. Or worse, one finds Judy Chicago inviting lush genitalia onto a plate, calling that Dickinson, choked by stiffened rings of lace that orbit to the edge of the porcelain—and to the end of our patience— for cliché and inordinate piety. Earlier, in the forties, Martha Graham had put her dance troupe to honoring the poet in her "Letter to the World." Louise Bogan, writing to critic Morton Zabel on the performance, was already adamant: ". . . all these probings into the soul of Emily Dickinson are tripe. . . . The really interesting things about her are too silly or too tragic to be danced. . . . Martha Graham," she added, "is nuts."

Since the fifties, when Dickinson's surviving letters and poems were finally collected, the quality of the homage, at least among scholars, has shifted somewhat. No, the reigning biographer Richard Sewall assures us, she was not out of her mind—not, as some have claimed, a psychopathological case. She chose her solitude consciously, and if this were done with sorrow, one understands through both the letters and the poems it was a coherent sorrow, joy evident in that lucid control. Sanity may suggest craftsmanship, which may in our minds suggest real distance between art and life. Yet emphasis remains on a personal revelation: what was the "terror" she spoke of entering her life in 1861, which if not the cause of her retreat, did nothing to prevent it? Alternate theories have not completely replaced the earlier fever to "find the lover" who scorned or was scorned. Was it *Springfield Republican* editor Samuel Bowles or Clergyman Wadsworth, or the old favorite, Judge Otis Phillips Lord? And why this nagging commitment to the fairy tale's monogamous center? Rebecca Patterson led the case for another lover, Kate Anthon, whom the poet met at twenty-eight. Or was Dickinson decidedly, passionately chaste, the perpetual girl-child, a virtual Peter Pan of Amherst?

All these palpitations absorb yet finally diminish, immediately rich but thinning rapidly as neighborhood gossip. What good does it do us? Perhaps it is the whole set we want, all the exotic staging, the depth and despair of context, the operatic fury of years we imagine furious because the poems are exactly that, and so—dogged prosaic monsters that we are—we connect a human life to them. We're used to Whitman, after all, and his loose abundant migrations. We come to Dickinson's work as we come to stones, circling that elegant density with both awe and annoyance, benighted and lit by its private weight. Here is a poet who had the nerve and invention to want what is nearly impossible: to record, as she wrote Thomas Higginson in 1862, that "noiseless noise in the Orchard." We enter the poems to hear it and through that deepening landscape the town, the house, the room. Perhaps all elegiac focus is egocentric at heart; we want only to *recognize*, which is to say, to see ourselves, our century in the work, and thus find footing, as if our own ambitions were at stake.

Such grounding is much simpler with Whitman, who is, in his way, the ebullient antagonist, brilliant sidekick and costar with Dickinson in that movie we are only a grandmother away from, the nineteenth century. What was it, Robert Hass has asked, that made men actually *hear* differently? Whereas earlier, rhyme and meter had held the "power of incantatory repetition," now they seemed mere "monotony." Whitman, bursting unaccountably from his forgettable half-life in hack journalism, eked out a line that itself, like some berserk divining rod, echoed the roar and rupture of the time, the country pulled west as if by lunar force, vast immigrations multiplying and confusing culture. So much plain doing in *Leaves of Grass*: Guy Davenport once observed violent movement as the center of the work, an age of wrenching turns and strains by buckboard and carriage, by horseback and the new lurching narrow-gauge trains. Whitman with his relish for the individual and the mob worked his famous persona as a camera works, with detail and anonymity, inventing the appropriate embrace for energy that would compress on itself *as city*, the major and ungovernable image of our century. In offhand reverence for this we call him *modern*, grateful for his populous, emphatically joyful hallucination. It is the darker side of our spirit that still hungers, some need to foil this public, extravagant vision. Thus the incessant pilgrimage to Amherst which has not stopped since that house came available to strangers some twenty years ago.

The door opens perhaps too easily, for in a way closer than Whitman to that century, Dickinson kept as much as she could bear to the old appearances, the familiar sequence of common meter, not wrestling down the whole structure as Whitman tried, but insisting on small changes: an interior wall here—or there, a window where a door once was. Much rhyme and off rhyme persists though she scanned fitfully, sometimes not at all. Occasionally she dismissed the whole matter into something close to free verse: the eccentric, spoken rhythms we so often find in her letters. Against the conventional poetry of the *Springfield Republican* or *Scribner's Monthly*, both of which she read, she was dissonance itself. Higginson advised her to conform, to give up her "spasmodic" gait. "You think me 'uncontrolled,'" she wrote back with embarrassment and bravado. "I have no Tribunal." To ears tuned to "Over the river they beckon to me— / Loved ones who've crossed to the further side; / the gleam of their snowy robes I see, / But their voices are drowned in the rushing tide," lines from a piece by Nancy Priest in the *Springfield Republican* in 1859, the following ones written by Dickinson three years later might seem close to heresy:

> There's been a Death, in the Opposite House,
> As lately as Today—
> I know it, by the numb look
> Such Houses have—alway—
>
> The Neighbors rush in and out—
> The Doctor—drives away,
> A Window opens like a Pod—
> Abrupt—mechanically—
>
> Somebody flings a Mattress out—
> The Children hurry by—
> They wonder if it died—on that—
> I used to—when a Boy— . . .

Such language, with its "spasmodic gait," seems to loom by comparison, the thinking—this was poetic taboo—terribly common, which is to say, realistic, stark. To our idea of things simmered now almost seventy years in more open forms, Dickinson's sense of line in this poem, and in so many others, may grate, nearly threatening intelligence with its ringing singsong, off rhyme or no. (It has been said—sweet hyperbole— that every Dickinson poem could be comfortably set to "The Yellow Rose of Texas.") The difficulty is in getting through the cultural debris between us, past the posturing of some of her work, its coy bruised tone picked up from popular verse; past that century's passion for biblical detail; past her tendency, especially in later years, to aphorisms and sentimental wisecracks ("Not at Home to Callers / says the Naked Tree /

Bonnet due in April / Wishing you Good Day"); and past—most of all—our own arrogance and impatience.

We can start again as she was fond of starting, from her "flood subject": death. In a life well known for control it is not surprising that her own funeral was planned as scrupulously as she put down her recipe for black cake or gingerbread. She wanted her coffin carried not by friends but by family workmen, six Irishmen who tended her father's orchard and meadow and lawn. She would have nothing of the street, asking to be borne out the back door, through the garden and the barn, then through three fields to the Dickinson plot, always with the house in view. Sewall tells us that a family friend, Clara Newman Turner, writing later of that day, claimed, with a sentiment already participating in legend, that the meadows were *"filled"* (her italics) with buttercups and daisies standing as "sentinels," bowing their heads as the group passed. Dickinson had been in a coma for two days. Her last letter, written to the Norcross cousins in early May, bore two words, "Called back," which were to be half of her tombstone inscription: *Called Back, May 15, 1886.*

That this phrase was also the title of a best-selling novel by Frederick Fargus—printed in London in 1884, pirated almost immediately in America, and nearly as popular as *Uncle Tom's Cabin* had been, selling by the next year nearly a quarter of a million copies—was not coincidence. Dickinson must have read *Called Back* in 1884, for she wrote to Louise and Frances Norcross early the next year, praising the story as a "haunting" one, "greatly impressive to me." She urged her cousins to read it, along with Holmes' *Life of Emerson,* though a vast gulf distanced the two books. Fargus' novel was trash. Even at the time, critics for the *Spectator* found *Called Back* "decidedly inferior," and the *New York Times* spoke of it as the stuff "that fills the columns of the cheap weeklies with fantastic stories, illustrated by dreadful cuts." It's not surprising that Dickinson, "for prose," took up Ruskin, Emerson, Emily Bronte, and Revelations; and "for poets," bypassing Whitman (who, she was told—and believed without reading—was "disgraceful") kept Keats and Browning and Shakespeare. But she had, in addition, at least in her last years, her pulp romance, her beach book. That this fact both loosens and deepens the poet—at least for me—is puzzling and welcome.

How trashy was this novel? Badly written in the barest technical sense, with tenses slipping crazily from past to present and into the past again, *Called Back* ferries its dull, excitable characters from England to Italy to Siberia and back in a gasping, confusing weave. Murderers live here, usually scarred and Italian, and the novel opens with its hero, Gilbert Vaughan, denying vile rumors about himself. No, he's not a communist, nor is he Roman Catholic. Swoons figure highly in the book, crucial, climactic really, in that each marks a stage in the budding consciousness of the narrator's near zombie bride, poor beautiful Pauline. Pauline has suffered a "shock," which is to say, some unspeakable experience has numbed her memory, reducing her to docile but cheerless idiocy. That such an event might have altered her virgin status of course preys upon our narrator, and everything moves fitfully to the most powerful scene in the story, one that I suspect Dickinson held for quite a while in her head and probably admired. Naturally, all hangs on Pauline, on the mysterious grindings of her most private intelligence. Rising from one of her final near fatal swoons, she walks trancelike, leading Gilbert into the seediest section of London where, in a dark walk-up, we find ourselves on the verge of the miraculous. Pauline passes out at once and instinctively the narrator grabs her hand: *illumination*, sudden and incomprehensible. Before him, flooded with light, in tableau, is the wrenching scene itself: a murder, with Scarface still wielding the knife aloft; the young male victim prone in handsome agony; the accomplices—up, left, and center—stilled as ice. Gilbert drops her hand and all is night, empty as before. He takes it up again, and yes, the monstrous frozen moment recurs. Dark and light, separation and the touch of hands—the narrator cannot replay this clairvoyant trick enough.

Dickinson was past fifty, certainly not a kid anymore. But in loving this, as her letter suggests, she was not alone in her regard. Around her, interest was rising in the mysteries of human comprehension though psychology was a relatively new science, its first lab established in Leipzig by Wilhelm

Wundt only five years earlier and Freud still fifteen years from the publication of his *Interpretation of Dreams*. In literature, this translated into an increased gesture toward the occult, particularly by popular novelists like Fargus, whom *Blackwood's Magazine* singled out with a kind of horror as "the boldest of all in his adoption of those powers which so many people begin to believe in, and which it is fashionable to say are not supernatural at all, but depend upon some inexplicable action of the mind. . . ." The narrator of *Called Back* sums up the infamous scene described above by telling us, "That is what Pauline saw, what she perhaps was seeing now, and what, by some strange power, she was able to show me as one shows another a picture."

One shelters Dickinson's love for this silly, melodramatic book, and something stirs: loss that shows itself as physical presence, a past that remains immediate forever. In the novel's hideous tableau we are face to face with pure image, without the irrelevant trappings of explanation or conclusion. William Carlos Williams once remarked that we praise in Dickinson the wrong things, "her rigidity of the sleepwalker, the rapt gaze, the thought of heaven." He advised us to look elsewhere, to her "structural warping . . . the distress marking the places at which she turned back. She was a beginning," he wrote, "a trembling at the edge of waking— and the terror it imposes." Consciously or not, she managed to shatter and distill the lyric, anticipating our century even as Whitman was making glittering mincemeat of narrative, redefining the epic.

Dickinson's nerve *is* that original in both matters of timing and attention though probably in the end these two are the same, a substance. In her best work she pulls up short, the air so electric that we hardly know anymore this is a poem we have entered. We could say the poem witnesses; it is not a message—nothing is *carried* in the conventional sense. Carefully the poem builds as intense experience does, nearly forcing us out of our lives, out of any control we might imagine.

"I heard a Fly buzz—when I died—" she begins in her studied offhand way, which shocks by its unlovely attention to an insect so self-absorbed and ubiquitous that a small dark horror immediately surrounds us. Against this is "stillness," deepened by the fly's grating repetitions, but deafening because it predicts disaster. We are adrift and diminished by the sound. It was *like* the air's stillness "Between the Heaves of Storm." Through the next two stanzas, Dickinson surveys everything expertly, with cinematic cool: the mourners' eyes, past tears; their breathing, now returning to normal; everyone's purposeful, peaceful abandonment. The watchers wait, as convention dictates, for the soul's release, "for that last Onset—when the King / Be witnessed—in the Room." The speaker too has been responsible and punctual, already having "willed my Keepsakes—Signed away / What portion of me be / Assignable." All this legalistic smoothing only stalls the poem, distracts us from melancholy by its understatement and brief wit. We are almost elsewhere, busy with the dullest kind of busyness, when we are trumped again: ". . . and then it was," Dickinson drops her news, "There interposed a Fly." This is superb timing, which clinches and continues to undercut itself. It is no longer simply the fly called up by the initial image, but a fly "with Blue—uncertain stumbling Buzz." It gains in horror, overextending itself, lurching in a kind of misdirection, magnified "Between the light—and me—" darkening everything. "And then," the poet manages, "the Windows failed—and then," she adds, breathlessly now, to get the story out, "I could not see to see—" The poem, in spite of the finality of the ending rhyme, seems, by the hurried dash, to break off in midsentence, terrible and incomplete. In short, it is modern, having no truck with larger, finer orchestrations out to make us believe in something, that would tie up immensity with a bow.

Perhaps it is odd that this, one of Dickinson's most surprising poems, remains one of the few everyone seems to know, anthologized to death with mealy choices like "I'm Nobody! Who are you?" and "There is no frigate like a book," pressed into the swimming unconscious of literate Americans, sixth graders to grandmothers. The poem focuses closely, almost myopically, on unnerving but natural things: the sound of a fly, its eerie gyrations, the nature of light. Her detachment seems almost scientific in the twentieth-century sense, for though she studied with Edward Hitchcock, Amherst College's charismatic Professor of Natural Theology and Geology, and was guided by his careful scrutiny of physical detail, she tended to underplay his religious conclusions. Most out of sync with the century's poetic habits is her conscious movement away from the typical imagery of death. Recall Nancy Priest of the *Springfield Republican*, speaking glibly of snowy robes and rivers, rushing tides to be crossed. Instead, Dickinson is rigorous and realistic, concentrating narrowly—with a brilliance that approaches iridescence—on peripheral things: not death, the grand abstraction, but much closer, the small annoyances that rattle and rage until they kill. In interview with David Hamilton, Donald Hall spoke outright on this point and he might as well have been commenting on Dickinson's poem: "Peripheral vision is where the symbols are." In our age, where the old weighty dazzlements—fate, life, truth, and so on—inspire denial or, at worst, boredom, Dickinson emerges with this visual, surface stance. Mute, contemporary.

Of course, in much of her work the heady abstractions of her age still compel. As ambitious as Whitman really, she hinged whole poems on such verities in a fever to elevate and define. "'Hope' is the thing with feathers—" Dickinson wrote, and in a play at self-defense, "I cannot live with You / —It would be Life— / And Life is over there— / Behind the Shelf." She does, in fact, slip too easily into philosophy. Yet against the trumpeting methods of the day, she separates herself by compression and invention. Kate Carlisle's lines on an apocalyptic theme in *Scribner's Monthly* in 1875 do worse: "And Truth shall conquer, Love shall reign, / Truth without harshness, Love without stain; / But we shall not see it—Thou and I / We are weak and weary; we shall lie / In that blessed cool blue dark of the sea, / Joyless and Moanless, safe and free. . . ." Contrary to such pretentious habits, Dickinson shoots low and fresh to bottom-weight metaphor, focusing, however oddly, on *things*, as Williams would later have it, both real and common. "My Life had stood—a Loaded Gun," she tells us, dropping then so deeply into analogy that we lose sight of who or what the speaker is, the initial connection. By the poem's end, the gun is thoroughly sentient and strange, its power funneled through such violent calm ("I'm deadly foe—" the speaker tells us, in a threatening aside, "None stir the second time— / On whom I lay a Yellow Eye— / Or an emphatic Thumb—") that we forget—then remember, startled—it is some dark inner substance in human experience she speaks of, something as unstoppable as the riddle that ends the soliloquy. "For I have but the power to kill," she writes, "Without—the power to die—"

The imagery in this poem—animated, though certainly not cartoonish—carries us off into another landscape entirely, where enormous leaps are inevitable, where guns speak and the flaming bullet is a "yellow eye." We might label this approach *surreal*: an evenness of tone before a situation turned inside out, a pretense at logic against shocking turns in description. Sometimes a single line or two will do it in Dickinson's poems. "Not all Pianos in the Woods / Had power to mangle me—" Or more well known: "I felt a Funeral in my Brain, / And Mourners to and fro / Kept treading—treading—" Or more wonderfully, she writes ". . . of larger—Darknesses— / Those Evenings of the Brain— / When not a Moon disclose a sign—" With lines like these, we are back to her amazing habits of attention: her brilliance at metaphor, and the dark solitude in her that keeps whimsy from overtaking, say, the "Pianos in the Woods" image, holding it quiet until the crush of the word "mangle" steadies things. Her composure could easily lull, and thus blind us to the stunning discovery of such connections, her sense that a poem must be immediate, not so much a recollection as a presence itself. After all, she wanted to know (and asked the *Atlantic* editor Higginson) not if her poems made sense either metrically or rationally, but if they were "alive," if they "breathed."

In view of her full work, which Higginson knew only in part, the questions are natural enough, but pressed next to the leaden ambitions of her contemporaries, they appear nearly incomprehensible. "Some Recent Women Poets," an editorial comment in *Scribner's Monthly*, ran in 1885, when Dickinson was forty-five. Even for Elizabeth Barrett Browning, that "apostle of the true woman's poetry," the article declared, "health was not the prominent characteristic." Sadness was to be the female objective, just as men sought to "preserve the most joyous side" of life. What we have, the essay continued, is "a boudoir poetry. . . . It is woman amusing herself—now with flowers, now with a momentary doubt and darkness, elegant in tone, and sometimes graceful; but so indefinite in her aims as to seem idle. . . ." Dickinson, reading this as she probably did (its editor J. M. Holland and his wife Mary were family friends), must have felt marooned indeed. Either that, or amused.

I'd go with amused, for by then Dickinson must have been well aware of her range as a poet. "Boudoir" poet perhaps, but only at times, and always with an air clear and chilling. Richard Sewall has made much of her grasp of the physical world, her knowledge of chemistry and botany and geology. Certainly her training in geography and history, coupled with the nineteenth-century mania for travel books, increased her imaginative terrain east to India, south to Peru, and north as far as Russia, with some eighty points between. The breadth of her subject matter, however, is less formidable than the complexity of her states of mind, the emotional intelligence that governs the poems. Marianne Moore, for one, admired her not for her grief nor for her passionate scrutiny of love and nature (though she echoes Dickinson's shrewd attention to the physical world), but for her wit. Laurence Stapleton tells us what Moore recorded in her notebook at Bryn Mawr. "In Irony," she wrote, "the pt. is to keep your temper and not fall into invective." She placed Dickinson next to "Hooker Swinburne James" in this, though of the four, Dickinson probably makes the most obvious effort at keeping temper, and perhaps this is exactly what Williams praised in her, a "distress" that marks the places where she "turned back." In such a reading, impatience surfaces in her violent dashes, and in her insistence on sentences unfinished or so clustered with images we nearly lose track. Against that, irony lets her unconventional vision loose, and brings clarity. "We—Bee and I—live by the quaffing—" she declares, beginning in a rather uncharacteristic hail-fellow-well-met Shakespearian burst. "'Tisn't all *Hock*—with us— / Life has its *Ale*— / But it's many a lay of the Dim Burgundy." In the second stanza's brilliant play, purposefully glib rhetorical questions, arch and starry as knives, cross and buoy up the more cautious asides to step forward—one almost *sees* this—and let go like revelers in a bizarre ad-lib chorus line, a delight which continues to the poem's end:

> Do we "get drunk"?
> Ask the Jolly Clovers!
> Do we "beat" our "Wife"?
> I—never wed—
> Bee—pledges this—in minute flagons—
> Dainty—as the tress in her deft Head—
>
> While runs the Rhine—
> He and I—revel—
> First—at the vat—and latest at the Vine—
> Noon—our last Cup—
> "Found dead"—"of Nectar"—
> By a humming Coroner—
> In a By-Thyme!

Dickinson's mockery of such questions—"Do we 'get drunk'?"—and her attempt here to recover a delicious drunken state by jokes and camaraderie may have been, beyond the dazzling poetics, her answer to the turgid moral vicissitudes raking America midcentury. Years before the Women's Temperance Union formed in 1874, Boston's Society for the Promotion of Temperance was spreading its fervor in six thousand local chapters; its effect in Amherst seems inevitable. Dickinson, however, was already suspect, for unlike almost everyone she knew, she steadfastly refused to be "saved"—a notable accomplishment in the Connecticut Valley where, in her lifetime, she withstood three great whirlwinds of revivalist campaigning. Her refusal was particularly daring, considering—as Cynthia Griffin Wolff does in her biography—that for a woman, conversion was "a sign of maturity" capable of endowing her "with a socially acknowledged adult identity that was independent of both father and husband."

Her ironic edge, however, is often quieter, closer to despair and its necessary inventions; sometimes it emerges with a folksy, funny—again, surrealistic—move toward a narrative of clever, elaborate disguise. "I started Early—Took my Dog— / And visited the Sea— / The Mermaids in the Basement / Came out to look at me." Beyond this rather mythic if not epic beginning, we find a complex description of near death by water—or love (". . . the Tide / Went past my simple Shoe— / And past my Apron—and my Belt / And past my Bodice—too")—which ceases only because "the Solid Town" intervenes and turns back the sea in questionable rescue. With her black whimsy, Dickinson deliberately plays down what other writers might easily have rushed to tragic heights.

Do we believe her—this poet for whom even heaven is "a small town" kept aloft by a single ruby? American poets do believe with affection, and rivalry. Robert Frost, whose own poems suggest her dark pendulous rhythms crossed with a similar eccentric turn of language and image (put, say, "One Need not be a Chamber—to be Haunted" next to "Desert Places" or "Directive"), zoomed in—according to Reginald Cook—on her minute infractions of word choice for those listening at Breadloaf in 1964: "'Parting is all we know of heaven, / And all we need of Hell.' . . . And all we *need* of hell. That's another word, you see. She doesn't say 'know' of hell; she says 'need.' Wonderful that 'need' in there. Sometimes you get a thing like that in your head and it dawns on you." John Berryman would invite her by name into his *Dreamsongs* with typical rowdy relish. "Them lady poets must not marry, pal. / Miss Dickinson—fancy in Amherst bedding her," he sings in #187, though later, in *Love and Fame*, he was, if not repentant, at least more fair. "But dividends too: / Miss Bishop, who wields a mean lyric / since Emily Dickinson only Miss Moore is adroiter." For Anne Sexton, Dickinson was somewhat closer to the legend, the sainted mother who purified poetry by her disinterest in publication, an option Sexton suggested to a beginning poet anxious to send to magazines. "Emily Dickinson," she argued in her letter, "never bothered with the whole thing. She was content to write them." Sylvia Plath, whose own work seems—as Williams said of Dickinson's—to be "trembling at the edge of waking," too near that "terror," cited her in her journal as a poet whose reputation foreshadowed her own. Robert Francis wrote such a passionate dialogue with Dickinson, set in darkness near the Amherst Commons, that upon hearing him read it in 1976 the audience at the town's Jones Library fell into laughter, sure that the poet was ironic. Francis stopped short, and began his poem "Two Ghosts" again, for embarrassed if not more patient listeners.

R. *Someone is here. Angelic? Or demonic?*
E. *Someone less than someone.*
R. *Emily?*
E. *How could you divine me?*
R. *An easy guess, you who were ghost while living and haunting us ever since.*
E. *A ghost to catch a ghost?*
R. *A poet to catch a poet. . . .*

Theodore Roethke's biographer, Allan Seager, tells us that he, Roethke, so hungered for her that he nearly lost himself, or so a young Stanley Kunitz warned him, finding far too much "feminine delicacy and precision" in his first book, *Open House*.

On and on the homage continues by reference or explanation, or more directly by imitation, until it seems something crucial to our survival to remember her, something the Chinese know by their hurried care, in the hours following a death, to put out food for the new ghost, to appease its inevitable anger at such abandonment. In unmarried women it is said the rage is enormous, nearly unquenchable; not properly belonging to families by birth, but only by marriage, such women are most acutely orphaned, and may—if not soothed—turn terrible mischief on those left behind: drownings, fires, marital disruptions, suicides. *Hungry ghosts*, they are called. And the small tables heaped with gleaming colorful vegetables and steaming chicken outside the mourning houses are not mere gestures of hospitable provision, but calculated stays against danger.

Such danger, nevertheless, and certainly such hunger, are what serious writing, particularly poetry, honors. The strain and silence in Dickinson's best work suggest something not finally and perfectly etched, but willfully incomplete, broken off—sometimes violently. Her power is costly, and continuing, because it seems only partly visible, yet for all that believable to us, compelling us forward, a curious machinery with its immediate, eternal spins and hums. As for the food we leave out for her—one hundred years now of flattering concern and delicious sidestep—only *our* appetite has increased. "Great Hungers feed themselves," Dickinson wrote at fifty to her sister-in-law, Susan Gilbert, "but little hungers ail in vain." No doubt we worry too much about this ghost.

Poetry and Its Rubble

First my brother took me there, a place that only half stood, rising on a bluff, the bluff itself worn back by decades of the lake's blue pounding—not like the ocean with its hard salt but deadly toward the land just the same. Twenty-some years ago we sleepwalked from the car into its weird half-life, high and regal on the bluff—Colonel McCormick's mansion—built when? 1920? 1928? My brother wasn't sure. The certain thing was rumor: the gnarly, bigoted editor of the *Chicago Tribune* had turned sweet for a year building the place we squinted at—massive rooms still, and halls on this pitch of land over Lake Michigan's dizzying expanse. A mansion for his wife, a girl really, decades younger than he. We made our way through the roofless ballroom, out toward more ordinary rooms, half underwater. The story was just the kind young girls themselves repeat, and no less tragic for its sentiment and cliché. She died there, everyone said, the second year, hung herself for whatever dark reason. And McCormick locked the door behind him, refusing to sell, *willing* that, so even after his death only poplar and quick maple and scrub kept at it through the roof and wall, some squatters in good weather, and always the lake, grinding its slow trance over the place, getting closer, claiming more each year. Pretty corny, my brother said, being older. But our awe survived our scorn for melodrama. We wandered and poked around the fallen stones, the wainscoting, stained and split. I could hear the lake, the reliable push and pull of water, the dipping stupid gulls. Walking around like that, what were we doing? Occasion for curiosity, for half-reverence, for disbelief—the very hopelessness filled us with odd, edgy promise. That, of course, was imagination at work.

❦

Watching things go to rubble, and by such attention, honoring stray bits and leavings—perhaps this has always been the major cottage industry of poetry, that first recycler. Certainly loss, and its sweet counterpoint, longing, have been the tonal crossbeams in verse since the beginning, a seriousness that has withstood all manner of cheapening, one particular trying form a gardening fad in the eighteenth and nineteenth centuries to inspire contemplation, if not poems, the wealthy routinely erecting new stone towers and walls on their estates, new things made to *look* ancient, crumbling done with a hammer, walls unfinished, all set far enough from the house, the sight vague but clear enough for gazing and dreaming, minutes at a time. Our eternal *ruinenlust* Rose Macaulay has called it. But certain poets, say, Goldsmith in his deserted village, or later, Wordsworth in his graveyards, Hardy in his, wrote to something larger, death let into poems as meditative backdrop and certainty, not a mere character with influence. Death in the year's cycle too—"Romantic poets are bothered by Autumn. . . ." That is Wallace Stevens, the great abstracter, and certainly one is struck by how often poets have allowed themselves to be drawn by that particular season, its palpable decay. "Dead leaves crushed grasses fallen limbs," wrote W. S. Merwin some twenty years ago, "the world is full of prayers." These things so mortal invite metaphor though what we witness is more process than thing, a thing on its way to something else, an experience as banal as it is miraculous.

But the presence of strictly human-made wreckage—old places on crumbling bluffs, or things seen almost daily like wrecked cars in the city or beyond, off country roads, abandoned barns falling into themselves—these come back to bother us in quite another way. Before the First World War, it was a German sociologist, George Simmel, who took up the subject, speaking brilliantly of ruins in spite of his colleagues who considered the subject trivial. The ruin, he argued, is somewhere between the "no-longer" and the "not-yet" though an object of profound peace, hence our fascination and pleasure with it. The force of human beings, *our spirit*, is always rising, literally with stone and arch and pillar; it is met and broken down by nature—weather and time—and where the struggle ceases, or at least slows, we have a line of rest, tragic but not sad, in part because—and these are Simmel's words— "the ruin creates the present form of a past life." More, by standing before such worn out places, or holding some small broken thing in hand, in that stillness—Simmel again—"we command in spirit the entire span of time since its inception." The McCormick mansion delivered awe to us. Part of that was its terrible legend. But even anonymous places—teetering farmhouses where one ignores the "no trespassing" signs— hold equal treasure. Abruptly one comes upon them: water-stained roses climbing up the wallpaper over the yellowing filthy sink. Or as a friend of mine said once at a backyard sale, moved by the homemade wicker weave on a damaged rocker: *someone had a plan for this.*

What else are images then, but evidence of such plans? Early in Theodore Roethke's poem "The Far Field," we're called into a place of great secret, a "corner missed by the mower" where mouse and catbird nest, near the "ever changing flower dump." But as we approach the real wealth of that stanza, as more living, organic elements are left behind, the pace quickens, given over to harder debris and harder, more urgent music—the first stress trochaic, spondaic sounds which tighten toward, and trigger revelation. "Among the tin cans," Roethke writes, "tires, rusted pipes, broken machinery, / One learned of the eternal . . ." What's telling is the litany—tires, rusted pipes—an elegiac sound that would stay with Roethke for years. All that junk behind his father's greenhouse.

❦

Imagery, of course, is not an end but an active means, and perhaps our wrecks, our orphaned things, most eloquently suggest this even as they imply a particular approach to poems, a kind of staring really, as if to call up the simplest questions, not only of form, but, because we're talking about its breakdown, something in the larger realm of being. *Among*—and I emphasize that word—"Among the tin cans," Roethke wrote, almost companionably. Quickly we are into matters of shape, forms breaking down, becoming something else; we're close to the body, to daily exertion and exhaustion. Such a physical thing, the shape of human thinking in a poem, which finally *is* the poem, however broken and incomplete.

Robert Frost's poem "Directive" keeps coming back to me in this physical way, possibly because its mysteries from the beginning orbit around collapse: the loss of old New England villages, their roads, their farms; we witness what is left—"forty cellar holes," a near total disappearance that simple nostalgia—making up, say, "a cheering song of how / someone's road home from work this once was"—neither comforts much nor resolves. The tone, like much of Frost, is cranky and smart and distracted. But the poem's shape—and here I mean syntax, how its sentences jump and blur and spark—seems dreamily removed from most of his work which tends to move on the force of statement, a thesis ready to be worked out, however conversationally, through the half-soothing meter and rhyme of its argument. In "Directive," all that clarity is dismissed, the argument already thrown out by the hopeless monosyllables of the first line; we come in *after* the fact somehow. "Back out of all this now too much for us, / Back in a time made simple by the loss / of detail, burned, dissolved, and broken off / Like graveyard marble sculpture in the weather. . . ." When Frost finally gets to the point—the initial point anyway—it comes eerily stripped-down, a kind of nursery rhyme or riddle. "There is a house that is no more a house / Upon a farm that is no more a farm / And in a town that is no more a town."

One could argue that's quintessential Frost, the simplicity almost mocking—thus underscoring—the complexity of loss. But what to make of the next long passage, the cutesy personification of landscape back to prehistory, the glacier that eons ago cut the town its quarry's "monolithic knees." Now the glacier is blown up to proper nounhood, his "feet stretched against the Arctic Pole." Frost's bit of corny romance is quickly undercut by an entirely different take on things, winding back to a human presence, the wonder of "two village cultures" and together, what they create. "Both of them," the poet blurts out, "are lost."

I'm not sure why "Directive" has stayed with me, or more accurately, to use Stevens' word again, has *bothered* me so long. It might be because the piece keeps abandoning itself, starting one way, dropping that for another habit of telling. How silly it gets for a while, veering off into straight description of trees and light, widening then to a little social history until even that attempt at meaning seems used up, the sorrow of it all too close perhaps to disguise with explanation or wit. It's as if Frost mimes the painful dissolution of his subject, discarding this approach and that, a line of well-intentioned clutter behind him until the poem—it does this—goes mute. The talkative Frost has run out of invention.

To my knowledge, he never spoke about the writing of this piece, not so directly at least as he did about "Birches" which also went dead in the middle. According to Brooks and Warren, who quote from a letter he wrote in 1950, that poem is "two fragments soldered together. . . ." It's easy to figure where. He got those young women drying their long hair in the sun, so much his dream of the long-leafed branches, the trees themselves: that must have stopped everything. When he did pick up "Birches" again, a great while later, the transition was half sheepish, half inflated, but the cadence of the phrase was all reason and self-assurance—"But I was going to say when Truth broke in / With all her matter-of-fact about the ice-storm . . ." The pause in "Directive" is interior, more chilling. "Both of them are lost"—and there we stall. I know of no other moment in Frost's work like this. I like to think I'm witness to the exact point where the poet lost sight of what he did, what he could do, the plan now in ruins.

"Directive" was a poem Frost didn't particularly like to read in public. Before audiences he was uncharacteristically diffident, saying how as some work was "more open," this one was "closed." "I'll do it slow and you take it straight," Reginald Cook quotes him telling one group at the Breadloaf School of English in 1955. "But it's all full of dangers, sideways, off. . . ." A year later, before another group there, he said outright,

"See, I don't read it with the same certainty that I should. I feel a little afraid of it. . . ."

It's that fear that haunts, and changes things. "Both of them are lost," Frost declares flatly of the two abandoned villages, meaning not only a village of course, but a world. What next? No breezy "But I was going to say . . ." will do here. This wonder's much too grim. Certainly we're at the end of something, waiting there, though that word—waiting—is far too calm. "And if you're lost enough to find yourself / By now, pull in your ladder road behind you. . . ." We go inward then, through that keyhole of stillness to a deeper level, Frost sounding so personal, and if we are to believe his public remarks, so unsure, that he scares himself.

The piece moves brilliantly from this moment on, all at a downward edgy angle. We're thrown back on the ruin—"some shattered dishes underneath a pine" where the children's playhouse stood, and the cellar hole again, now "belilaced." But taking everything in this specific way is to be there, to see such things. And the tone, no longer nostalgic, is immediate and urgent. We end with water, something underground, way below the house, a "destination" and a "destiny," and with a stolen playhouse cup—like the Grail, says Frost, "broken" and "under a spell so the wrong ones can't find it." We're asked to drink and drink. We're sent back to our sources, to whatever holds the greatest mystery for us. "Here are your waters and your watering place," the poet insists in his famous final sweep. "Drink and be whole beyond confusion."

When Randall Jarrell in 1947 wrote about *Steeple Bush*, the collection in which "Directive" appeared, he was coolly negative, dismissing it along with most of Frost's later books as full of poems having "few of his virtues, most of his vices, and all of his tricks." To Jarrell, the later work seemed a sort of rubble pile, evidence of "what was genius," persistent shards of "someone who once, and somewhere else, was a great poet." In *Steeple Bush*, however, he found a major exception. "But one stops for a long time at 'Directive,'" he wrote with uncharacteristic and melancholy reserve.

The way Simmel says we stare down and disappear into ruins: that is exactly how one looks at "Directive," steadily, watching it diminish until we are left only with our watching. Part of the human power of the poem is that it seems to fail. With its first half's false starts, then its second half's descent into the most fuzzy interior regions, all this grief-struck, world-weary meandering seems less the polished result of much effort than the painful effort itself. In this, it predicts much contemporary verse; one senses the stop and start of its making. More, like all great art, it feels uncertain, unfinished, its questions greater than its answers. Surely Frost must have been aware of this with his "I'm a little afraid of it" though he knew—and scorned—the way it was hailed by what he called the Eliot school of poets. "This is the poem," he told Elizabeth Shepley Sergeant in 1949, "that converted the other group. The one these fellows have taken to build my reputation on. The boys call it great. They have reestimated me. This is great and most of the rest, trivia." In spite of such public bravado, the mysterious privacy of that poem shines; the mind splinters against it. Years of rereading do nothing to change that.

Human experience is, of course, partial. I like to think this is why poems linger in the mind like smoke and seem true, because poetry too is partial, its ambition never to explain everything away and pretend a wholeness. Nor is it exactly to witness or to mirror though observation is prized, that chance to see those broken dishes in the abandoned playhouse for one lovely moment before they *mean* anything. Wallace Stevens talks about poetry's "transaction"—good lawyer that he was—and pictured a light fall of snow in Hartford. "It melted a little by day and then froze again at night, forming a thin, bright crust over the grass," he wrote. "At the same time, the moon was almost full. I woke once several hours before daylight, and as I lay in bed I heard the steps of a cat running over the snow under my window almost inaudibly. The faintness and strangeness of the sound made on me one of those impressions which one so often seizes as pretexts for poetry."

Two words to stress: *faintness* and *strangeness*, the cat imagined because it is never actually seen. So the mind floats there. Are there rational ways to think about such experience? And why is it a pleasure, the idea of Stevens awake in the dark bedroom listening this way, seizing upon this small useless sound of an ordinary cat on the icy moonlit snow outside? A *transaction*, Stevens said, between reality and the sensibility of the poet. Faintness and strangeness, he said. Poets in their invention have long been thought to be on the edge of language, at the forefront of perception, leading their more laggard siblings, those writers of reasonable worldly prose. In fact, I think that poets don't lead at all, but hang around on the edge of things, taking up whatever's dismissed or ignored—just a cat one night, less, the sound of a cat, or just a village no one alive even remembers—sensing the weight and tremble there, the fear. That, and something else.

❦

Joy then, in all this rubble too. Here's this: a June day, its light and leaf, the windows down in a friend's old van. We're giddy, yelling anything out to no one down the narrow ribbon roads that turn suddenly and we brake, gear down, to begin again. Western Massachusetts, and our friends are taking trash to the dump; we're singing our going-to-the-dump song, our precise and wayward doggerel. How close are we to "Directive," passing as we pass woods on either side, the stone walls worn down two centuries, maple and even oak towering over the spot where houses stood, and church and mill. But how far are we from what Jarrell called in that poem "so much longing and tenderness and passive sadness." This far in our joy, are we equally open to mystery? Not elegy now, as the van grinds and weaves, not that oldest of human utterances, but maybe the second oldest at this upward angle, the sweet what-the-hell of pure lyric, of song. This is the day we'll *get back* from the dump. My friends will find a huge bay window for their new back room, a monstrous thing, none of its hundred-some smaller panes shattered. We will lift it, altogether disbelieving, into the van, driving so carefully the dirt and gravel road home, amazed at those twin gods, dumb luck and happenstance.

Is there a way to measure joy? In poems, is there a kind of seismograph, something with wires and earphones whose fine needle will flicker and ride through the twists of syntax and image? "Day creeps down." That's the simple beginning of one of Wallace Stevens' most celebrated poems, "Man on the Dump." Full stop then, full sentence like a strand of pearls dropped suddenly on the rug. "The Moon," the poet says, "is creeping up." So we begin to rise, already in the half-daze and dark of memory. We're at the dump after all, altar of waste and abandonment, and unlike Frost, it's typical of Stevens not to mourn but to love this. "The moon is creeping up" he says, not the moon rising, not the moon already burned into place, but creeping—a word both *faint* and *strange*, that tentative secret ascent.

From there, we glide on the exuberant flashing of images. "The dump is full / of images" Stevens declares, opening to the confusing debris of twentieth-century life—"the janitor's poems / Of everyday, the wrapper on a can of pears / The cat in the paper bag, the corset, the box / From Estonia: the tiger chest for tea." The list could make us crazy, and it does, with Stevens caught up playfully in its orbit, things no longer quite themselves. Instead, they abstract themselves, all covered with dew. "How many men have copied dew / For buttons, how many women have covered themselves / With dew," Stevens asks. Is he serious? ". . . dew dresses, stones and chairs of dew, heads / Of the floweriest flowers dewed with the dewiest dew." Breathe now, count one, two, three after this absurd and lovely outburst. "One grows to hate these things," he says, "except on the dump." Stevens times this shift like some brilliant, offhand comedian, dropping tone as though the adult now, who, after all, has to remember things and think about dinner. But the excessive, goofy flight of that passage—we balloon out with it, nearly, like Stevens, losing ourselves in its music and play.

I suppose somewhere, someone has written a thorough sonorous gloss on all this "dewiest dew" and for the next stanza too, which winds its way, bumping along on its funny parenthetical asides. "Now, in the time of spring," Stevens nearly intones, *come to* from his rambling blip to focus upon "(azaleas, trillium, / myrtle, viburnums, daffodils, blue phlox), / Between that disgust and this, between the things / That are in the dump (azaleas and so on) and those that will be (azaleas and so on), / One feels the purifying change." And so the design of the thing begins to figure. Seen from the air how would the dump look? Shining cans and sad gray tires—the poet will speak of their "elephant-coloring" in a moment—and whatever ragged, broken this and that heaped up. But running along side is this explosive ring of color, spring flowers that will shake us out of our drab winter coma. In a climactic, theatrical turn, we have music too—not uncharacteristic this sort of "ta-dum" from Stevens—but it's cinematic here, the moon still on its creeping. Now the noisy backdrop—this "bubbling of bassoons" and the declaration, if not discovery that "Everything is shed; and the moon creeps up as the moon. . . ."

The moon then, just the moon, without our usual romantic baggage. Everything reduced to itself, this moment rare in Stevens, without metaphor, scaled down. In a way, we're back at Frost's great pivot of stillness in "Directive"—so much for the villages, "Both of them . . . lost." But how different is this world from Frost's, this sudden composure. Marianne Moore, in a typical fit of good sense, called Stevens a poet whose work was full of "multifarious plumage of thought and word . . . ," calling him "morosely ecstatic." It's point of view then, really a point of being, that makes him the ultimate "Un-Frost," not the morose part, but surely the ecstasy. Perhaps if we wished to boil things down to their little luminous nubs, we might say Frost and Stevens mark the opposite ends of poetic imagination in this century's first half, one morose and one ecstatic, both shot through with a keen sense of ruin. "The poet makes silk dresses out of worms," Stevens has written elsewhere, striking, as usual, his own eccentric take on one of our favorite clichés.

This openness to loss is part of the wonder in Stevens' "transaction," the element that makes the poem a place, an occasion really, where the inner world meets what is *out there*, worms and all. More clearly than in most of their other poems, both "Directive" and "Man on the Dump" imply an odd sort of pact with the great world, both pieces written in that slow armchair country overlooking massive public disasters—for Frost the Second World War and its ending nuclear slaughter at Nagasaki and Hiroshima; for Stevens, the poverty-struck days of the Depression. To say these are political poems, however—at least political in the urgent way we're used to these days—would be misleading. Instead, they work either the atmosphere or imagery of the times as an inner point of reference, Frost's hesitation and sadness in part due to his own complex feelings about nuclear power at the end of the war. According to biographers Thompson and Winnick, he, like others, believed the war over at last because of these weapons but he remained, nevertheless, uneasy even haunted by the horror of the outcome, the civilian deaths. As for Stevens, a poet so often accused of getting lost in the high private art of writing poems, an approach that would almost by definition dismiss any public brooding, "Man on the Dump" is a leap into the hard bottles and broken springs of things. Randall Jarrell's quarrel with him, for instance, that "he had every gift but the dramatic," that his poems lacked "immediate contact" with human detail giving themselves too easily over to philosophy, might be countered with it. "Stevens knows better," Jarrell himself admitted, "often for poems at a time."

This time, to be specific about Stevens is to follow him home to Hartford where in the early thirties he bought an expensive house just blocks from the city dump. In 1933, he wrote to his friend James Powers of the Russian refugees who had set up housekeeping on the edge of the dump itself. And it was his daughter, Holly Stevens, who has noted his particular fascination with a man there who had made himself a house of trash—crushed tin cans, boxes—staying for years and talking to almost no one. How all this turned slowly in the poet's mind clearly guides the imagery of "Man on the Dump" but its orbit goes wider. About this time, Stevens was asked to write an introduction for William Carlos Williams' *Collected Poems*, something he wanted to do for his old friend but in doing so, he defined something larger. "What, then, is a romantic poet now-a-days?" he asked.

> He happens to be one who still dwells in an ivory tower, but who insists that it would be intolerable except for the fact that one has, from the top, such an exceptional view of the public dump and the advertising signs for Snider's Catsup, Ivory Soap and

Chevrolet cars; he is the hermit who dwells alone with the sun and the moon, but insists on taking a rotten newspaper.

In a way, we're probably not too far from our nineteenth-century nobleman here, building on his property the while-you-wait ruins for contemplation and self-renewal. But we have a more serious commitment in the image of the hermit-poet, alone with the sun and the moon *and* the rotten newspaper; these contraries protect and guide. In the rest of his introduction, in his praise for the counterpoetic in Williams' work, Stevens set the standard, calling "essential" that poetry which thrives on "constant interaction of two opposites"— the "unreal and the real" or "the sentimental and the anti-poetic." In a later prose piece, written in 1946, Stevens raised a different set of contraries. "The role of the poet," he wrote, "may be fixed by contrasting it to that of the politician. The poet absorbs the general life, the public life. The politician is absorbed by it. The poet is individual. The politician is general." Necessary, thought Stevens, that the poet protect himself from what he called "the sabotage of the individual," protect, that is, "the personal" if he were to produce "significant poetry."

Meanwhile, back at the dump, we finally have a human being, cleverly disguised as all of us in his anonymous pronoun— "One sits and beats an old tin can, lard pail," Stevens tells us early in the ending stanza. "One beats and beats for that which one believes. / That's what one wants to get near." How many worlds collide in this moment: resignation, purpose, a hopeless joy? Such an ominous, almost comic roar in this solitary figure banging away, high on a heap of trash, surrounded by acres of fire-start rubble. It's the end of the world in such a vision, the last one of us with nothing but an old dented pail and a belief, some final shred of earnest thought. The stanza goes on, the sound itself the earnest sound of questions in spite of their half-whimsy. "Is it peace, / Is it a philosopher's honeymoon one finds / On the dump? Is it to sit among mattresses of the dead, / bottles, pots, shoes and grass and murmur *aptest eve* . . . ?" The moon not long ago was creeping up. Now the questions creep that way, the poem slowed and weighted by them even as we rise on their sound, our eye taken up to the grackles who "blatter" higher. The last question could break a heart with its unexpected plainness. "Where was it one first heard of the truth?" Stevens asks, no longer facetious at all. And then the final pronouncement—"The the"—more an amplification of the question than any solid answer.

So the poem is itself a standoff. But that Stevens' twisted, ornate, healing imagination found this image at all is an odd triumph and a massive sorrow both: a human being in the dump, the dump itself in the poem's dislocation, even the lard can, veteran of so many morning biscuits or pies nearly too sweet to eat, a matter of sudden mystery, a thing slipping free of ordinary time into quite another orchestration—a timeless, deeply meditative one, one that gives occasion for the longer, riskier view, which is to say *poetry*. "One beats and beats an old tin can, lard pail." For Stevens, an uncharacteristically simple utterance, this monosyllabic strain and stress, over and over. It's chant. But more. In the useless dignity of the dump, it's dirge.

How close the song is, this moment, to elegy; joy and sorrow in quiet collision. "Where was it one first heard of the truth?" Stevens asks—the question of icy nights, the faint strange sound of a cat running over the frozen snow outside, the question of an afternoon in woods when one comes upon the shattered remains of a kid's playhouse. Such things enter us and stay until we know by heart their flight and darkness. It's elegy we write, no matter what the poem or its place.

❦

Perhaps, then, a definition of poetry in any age depends on ruin, on how things taken apart by neglect and time and violence slowly come to be or refuse to be again, in poems. The latter, this refusal, seems more and more our uneasy method, our sacred grove not beautiful at all. The fractured places we find raise important questions of self and world that art always demands. The so-called Language poetry for instance—to enlarge Robert Hass' remark, made once at Wabash College, about Lyn Hejinian's book, *My Life*—might be gleaming shattered glass. Sentences in that book seem no longer sentences in the old coherence; instead we find fragments buried, phrases cut at inconclusive often lyric angles, a dense worldly but private rendering of a life. And that breathless fractured way comes alive in Jorie Graham's third and fourth collections, both in her lines and sentences which brutally—though not always—break off, unravel, repeat themselves senseless right before our eyes. In the more conventional voices among us—Galway Kinnell for instance, or in a reverse sort of urgency, Adrienne Rich—one still hears the heroic dream of narrative and announcement, a curious pageantry toward the high earned thing—love or change or something equally inspired—an equation in that rise, a conclusion. That sense of conclusion might well be romance, though what we often conclude these days is our own inability to conclude.

But it's more than that simple turnabout. What strikes me is the *public* way such uncertainty lives in American poetry. A useful example might be Philip Levine's work—I'm thinking especially of his long poem, "A Walk with Tom Jefferson"— which casts an inner survival against outer catastrophe, coming out, almost, in a draw. As urban in his vision as Frost was rural, Levine is, nevertheless, not far from Frost's abandoned roads and villages though the abandonment is partial, that scary on-the-verge-of. His Detroit scourged by fire and anger, neglect and greed—a wasteland minus Eliot's melodrama and self-pity—is still a place where one lives, the remarkable Tom Jefferson, an ancient black man who without apology or righteousness works his small vivid garden, his beans and corn and whatever else gives flowers and fruit, amid the burned out houses between (and here Levine sets nearly mythic boundaries) "the freeway and the ballpark." Shelter is no longer shelter except for Jefferson's house and a few others. One could dream, like Frost, of "someone's road to work this once was" but even to gear up in this standard romantic way is no longer the poet's business though one hears in Levine—as one hears in Frost—Wordsworth's perennial sigh and Keats' fitful, sleepless one.

It's all the junk Levine collects, those cast-offs that haunted Roethke behind his father's greenhouse. But it's all gone public, left on streets, overwhelming us in a larger, general way, the gutted gloomy waste of life and resource in this century, the "old couches and settees / burst open, the white innards gone gray . . . / yellow wooden / iceboxes yawning / at the sky, their breath / still fouled with years of garlic sausages and refried beans, / blue mattresses stained / in earnest, the cracked / toilet seats of genius. . . ." It's this debris that stirs us, its numb pathetic exposure against a spirit that is whole and human. "Dumping grounds," Levine calls this place against Tom Jefferson who opens his arms in irony to blocks of it. "We all came for $5 / a day and we got this!" he says, up from rural Alabama some fifty years before, a family with so many other families.

But in another way, we might never see, unless we squinted hard, Frost's ghost village here, its shattered broken dishes, its "house no more a house . . . in a town that is no more a town," "Directive"'s voice coming to us, such commentary, in the slow eternal aftermath where we stare down clues of lives once useful, ghostly boys and girls replaying play underneath a pine. It's distant; it's picturesque. Frost ends up disbelieving, though, past that, going inward, underneath the house for real water, too wily or too impatient even forty-five years ago to trust the imagination completely to such small sweet details. And of Stevens—another wayward line could be drawn from his dump to this, both touched by flowers ("azaleas and so on") against the sodden "mattresses of the dead," though Stevens' dump was always that, something, in Levine's world, a neighborhood tragically became. Still, the sacred plot between the freeway and the ballpark is troubling because it *keeps* troubling. It's not just aftermath but prophecy and immediate news. Those junked cars, their "slashed tires, / the insides drawn out of anything" and beyond them, the awful colors "blooming signs," Levine warns, of "all the earth we've pumped into the sky"—these are with us still; we *recognize* and see the beginning of our myths in them. *It's Biblical*, Tom Jefferson repeats over such waste and leavings, and over larger violence between parent and child, nation and nation. *It's Biblical*, a refrain that calls up Old Testament rage and justice, a silent, terrifying overview.

❧

This past year, late November, my brother took me to a second ruin, the first—the McCormick mansion—long leveled clean by lake and the petitions of angry neighbors. This one, an unofficial town park, was also private land—acres of open meadow and woods, with its battered "no trespassing" sign routinely ignored, the site, once, of a small unambitious amusement park in the thirties and forties. Embedded in the widest path were miniature trolley tracks. We could barely make them out, and as we walked, the twisted seats and motors, bent beams and crossbars of the rides themselves lay rusting in autumn light, in weeds. Here and there, not much of the angled junk—mostly woods, an occasional ornate stone pillar, inexplicable, in a line of trees.

What my brother loved most was the outdoor dance floor, and we followed him up the rise to find it, the size of an average backyard in the city, built flat and open against the hill. We found the broken light pole, flung down in the bare forsythia, and made the predictable leap, imagining dancers at night, beer in cold metal glasses, the cheap music that must have filled the park all summer. The floor was parquet, buckled now and rotted. Bits of it remained, oak cut at an angle and once laid cleverly, like a puzzle. But what struck us most was the spearmint—dense thickets of it on three sides, the leaves still green in spite of so many late night frosts, the scent piercing the cold air. Raspberry canes had grown through it like a maze; the thorny brambles scratched us, and caught our jackets, but we broke off leaves and shared them all around— three adults and two children—our mouths bitter and sweet with the spearmint's wild taste.

"No longer relevant" is a refrain in the final poem of Jorie Graham's third collection, *The End of Beauty*. "No longer relevant" she tells us, speaking of the body, or of love, in any case "one of the finished things, one of the / beauties, one of the forms (hear it click shut)." That clicking shut—one can feel the heart go numb with such a sound and know it true. Perhaps George Simmel's notion was only a pleasant dream, the darkened "no longer" sweetened and made new by promise, by the "not yet" in things. Graham's terrible phrase "no longer relevant," her "hear it click shut" is a click of will as well as heart, historical and personal at once. The strongest poetry of our century has such fear in it. And the strongest poems, always uncharacteristic, break to turn about, to resist—and often deeply stun—their makers. But this too: I know we biked that day, back to my brother's house, and well into evening, every now and then, the spearmint. . . . The kids had stuffed their pockets with it, and the oil hung for hours on our skin. Again and again in those ordinary rooms, someone would walk by or a hand would rest briefly on my shoulder, and I'd catch it—the quick, surprising scent of it—and stop.

Hopkins by Heart

It must have been the perfect size for death, that room in Dublin suspended for us now a century in early summer trees and streets. As children, we dreamt scenes like this, putting our thumbs over closed lids, and pressing. The place grays out, but here, the point of color—real—in that room, his mother's flowers sent from England, drawn carefully from their packet and revived in water. *Thank you,* Hopkins dictated, too weak to write; they are on my table now.

It took weeks, through May into June 1889, as the typhoid played out its poison. "I am a eunuch—" Hopkins had written a year earlier, at forty-three, to his friend Robert Bridges, "but it is for the kingdom of heaven's sake." By June 8th, his parents had arrived from England, two more in shadow, good Anglicans on watch awkwardly there amid the impossible, unthinkable Jesuits. How odd for them that place, and this man, nearly beyond them now. O nineteenth century and the overwrought beauty of your deathbed scenes. We are cool in our distance, embarrassed and suspicious of detail. But every biographer echoes this—Father Wheeler raising his hands for the last rites. And Hopkins whispering suddenly to no one in particular: *I am so happy, so happy.*

❦

Happiness. We are in an age that values something else: not pain exactly, but a painful, sometimes playful kind of scrutiny that makes for depth. Hopkins' happiness, if we can distill the poems down to that, is dizzy, radiant, outrageous, tender. It is monstrous. "The world is charged with the grandeur of God," he wrote—he told his mother, "in a freak" one day—"It will flame out, like shining from shook foil; / It gathers to a greatness, like the ooze of oil / Crushed. . . ."

Terrible. Triumphant. Things alight in their own opulence, violently into creation. At nineteen, Hopkins dazed himself pressing words back to their primitive lives—*Gr* sounds, so "onomatopoeic," he wrote in his journal. "Grind, gride, grid, grit, groat, grate . . . to strike, rub, particularly together . . . greet, grief. . . ." *Grief.* The word is chant and calls to itself for company. Grief, the low, welling member of the tribe, outlasting its triggering fact, the thing inside that grinds and grates, finally to break, or fly.

Such happiness is flight, or as near to it as a woman I know who dreams of flying. Night after night she dreams her friends around her, intent as doves, she tells me. They say to her, you can do it. They say, it's all in the small of the back. And slowly, flexing her spine low, just like that under their deep communion, she begins to move, lifts off, airborne, born of air. Departure, and *coming to.* Hopkins' poems are that: pure as pure light, strange as bird.

❦

From his journals. 1866. May 3rd. Hopkins is twenty-two, walking out into spring, that lush-everywhere green one imagines spring. Here, "a scarf of vivid green slanting away beyond the skyline," or there, "cowslips . . . bluebells, purple orchids." All the time, this *get everything*, this *see it.* And his companion, William Addis, talking as they walked of the fasting he vowed one summer, and silence, weeks of it, and of fainting on just such a walk. The poet moves on, hearing him, but thinking this: the hill "glistening with very bright newly turned sods," the elms and oaks creeping out "in small leaf." Meanwhile, Addis keeps talking, gregarious, unshakable in his story—such is the memory of his deliberate hunger. Yet this is hunger too: Hopkins scanning and taking in spring, its fertile, lovely indifference. He stands before such a world without interpretation. Feel the weight of this. It is awe.

❦

Awful then. In the old stunned version of that word. Or the version that mutely broods, real chimes that cut and cross the night—3 A.M., 4 A.M.—moving over the deaf, dumb sleepers to no consequence but hanging in the air like some sentient leaf. May 3rd once more. Addis talks on, bursting. But Hopkins keeps his eye careful, keeps at this humble greed to trace, reproduce, name. It is a garden he walks through. Early spring. The secret can no longer contain itself.

❦

A human secret too. Hopkins is so full of secrets—poems he burnt upon entering the priesthood ("the slaughter of the innocents," he notes in his journal), poems he held back the seven years before his final vows. Desires, decisions. Among the notes of summer 1867, days spent in trees, studying oak leaf and stem, inscape and instress, this mix he would name of form and spirit: "It was this night I believe but possibly the next that I saw clearly the impossibility of staying in the Church of England, but resolved to say nothing to anyone. . . ." And so one carries around a secret—this heavy thing that makes one weightless, hardly there at all. What is the body then? *I am not who you think I am. You are talking to someone else.*

❦

In some other time. So we invent Oxford of the 1860s, Hopkins' Oxford: all intricate disorder of religious doubt and leap, pose and counterpose, how to be loyal, the good Anglican—broad, low, or high church—or so high as to be dangerous, too close to Rome. And the feared loved tutors egging each their separate visions—Pusey, Liddon, Jowett—all powerful, all convincing. And there, the great convert himself, John Cardinal

Newman, still shimmering in his famous, infamous moment of conversion some twenty years before. It is he who will accept Hopkins into the Church and earn the poet's gratitude. "O Gerard my darling boy," his father wrote, utterly beside himself at the news, "are you indeed gone from me?"

Such moments clone themselves into ritual. One hundred years later, the 1960s are our equivalent wealth: campus pose and counterpose, astonishing changes, leaps and doubts of political—not religious—passion. How close we are to Hopkins in the riotous heart, the same bright tangled transparencies, one upon another in the old biology text—first the living nerves, then blood over the pale human figure, not patient at all under its thrilling disguise.

❧

First surprise: how the body knows before the mind knows. 1870. February. Hopkins recalls the Christmas retreat where hearing an account of the Agony in the Garden he began "to cry and sob and could not stop." Something doubles and divides—the one who grieves, the one who watches. What ghost is this that tethers out and looks back astonished? ". . . there is always one touch," Hopkins added, "something striking sideways and unlooked for . . . and this may be so delicate that the pathos seems to have gone directly to the body and cleared the understanding in its passage. . . ." Like geese, perhaps, which know the routes north and south, Georgia into New Hampshire, or west of that, up Arkansas into Illinois, past St. Paul all by heart, though not by living memory: a map in genes and buried cells, following, it is said, the ancient path the glacier took, though nothing must surprise those birds. But poets, yes, for poems somehow know their route and issue their demands by nerve. One feels poem—*body*—unfolding gradually, pressing itself into air and page until that moment the writer disappears. One participates in mystery then. *Mystery*, Hopkins argued to Bridges, is "an incomprehensible certainty," not *dogma*—the "dull algebra of schoolmen," a word people could "almost chew"—but something turned beyond curiosity, the mind "poised but on the quiver. . . ."

☙

August 24, 1868: "In the middle of, I think, this day . . . a piece of sky-blue gauze for butterfly-nets lying on the grass in the garden."

☙

The long retreat at Roehampton, September 1868, just two weeks after Hopkins' entry into the Jesuits at twenty-four. "I cannot promise to correspond," he had warned Bridges, "for in that way novices are restricted." It might as well have been Ignatius' cave he entered, his thirty days in retreat easily those bleak months three centuries before, Loyola at Manresa in 1522, the plague one day's journey off, in Barcelona, an almost palpable terror. Prayer, fasting, the terrible lush imaginings— all this Ignatius cooled, compressed, locked in his small, star- tling book, *The Spiritual Exercises*, around which orbits every mind that nears him.

"Blighty," the poet wrote of the weather, his only comment on the retreat's first day, "turning to fine." Imagine Hopkins then, imagining all that week and into the next and the next, in chapel darkness or on Roehampton's wooded paths, what the *Exercises* insisted: to *see* those miraculous events—the In- carnation, the Nativity, the Agony and Crucifixion—in all their fury, their garish breathless detail. So one flashes to keep up, making the mind a place not for ideas but for the brilliant surface: ". . . to form a mental picture," Ignatius urges for the Nativity, ". . . see . . . the road from Nazareth to Bethle- hem . . . consider its length and breadth, and whether it is level or winding through valleys and over hills." So Hopkins walks on, say, and the inner eye fills out the quiet human turmoil of the birth, what was whispered urgently or sweetly, every quick transparent gesture, the angle of light and fabric, the midwife's exhaustion; smells too, of the barn and the night, the low breath of animals gathered under the desert stars, suddenly cool after the leveling heat.

Where was Hopkins now? Roehampton? Was that possible? Careful Ignatius, crazed for the particulars of his affection, as a lover in memory plays out again and again the cherished scene until nothing, not real life, is quite so real. "Chestnuts," Hopkins notes in a day's single journal entry of those weeks, "as bright as coals or spots of vermilion."

❦

It was the training not so much of a priest, but of a poet. Images. Ways to keep the secret secret. Hopkins' journal, March 1871: "I have been watching clouds this spring, and evaporation, for instance, over our Lenten chocolate." On he continues, all intricate, questioning details—the look of gas bubbles ("grain on them"), the law of candle smoke, then back to those "bright woolpacks," the clouds themselves. "What you look hard at seems to look hard at you," he adds suddenly—though not, one suspects, in whimsy.

Tradition? "I have begun to *doubt* Tennyson," Hopkins at twenty confessed darkly to his friend A. W. M. Baille, and slowly one watches others fall aside: Browning, Matthew Arnold, Wordsworth. And later, to Robert Bridges—his greatest friend, shameless imitator, master of dull brilliance—in answer to his apparent plea that Hopkins, please, read more great work to override his bent for strangeness, the poet only shrugged. "The effect of studying masterpieces is to make me admire and do otherwise. So it must be on every original artist to some degree, on me to a marked degree."

❦

For Hopkins, it began on the page, in the rich speechlessness of childhood, but not in poems. Pencil, watercolor—the whole family kept the habit, generations of Hopkinses, Smiths, Manleys, a grandfather and uncles, aunts who would tutor him in drawing, cousins and brothers, amateurs, professionals. All knew how the body knows by line and color extending through

eye and brain and arm, spun through the split-second syn-
apses, cooling into the intelligent hand. More, the passion was
national in that century, a matter of class. To be educated was to
draw closely like the scientist, but devoutly, aware of some origi-
nating thought, though not a thought at all.

It was Ruskin, of course, in his sketch journals, and Cole-
ridge in his; at the lowest rung it was those awful well-
meaning ladies on tour, holding up their portable wooden
frames to make wilderness into landscape, to see it centered
and just-like-a-picture. But the time spent before trees and
sky and water was Hopkins' own, and survives in the sketch-
books, twenty-seven years' worth, the first begun at seventeen,
the last at forty-four, only days before his typhoid took. To
draw the way a wave *looks*, a stairwell, the turn of cliff or white
lily—this habit is patience, extinguishing the self to record the
miraculous event.

❦

And so in fever too, at least 103 those few days I remember,
pinned back in the flashing, mournful heat, the ceiling adrift
in its confusing, winding fissures. My husband's there, bring-
ing out poems from memory, poems he's stored up for years
in his body's darkness, holding them to my ear. Hopkins is a
bell, precise and blurring. I hear something—"dearest fresh-
ness"— something—this—"ah! bright wings."

❦

The Journals. 1872. St. Mary's Hall, Stonyhurst College,
Blackburn. "A goldencrested wren had got into my room at
night and circled round dazzled by the gaslight on the white
ceiling." So Hopkins too in flight leapt, dodged, caught the
creature in his hands, its heart pure terror. Bird eye to human
eye and the infinite bewilderment between. Is there an end to
such stillness? "Ruffling the crest . . . I smoothed and fin-
gered the little orange and yellow feathers. . . ." That night, it
was October and though the bird veered off, he woke to feath-
ers everywhere in the autumn room. In three days, his

brother Cyril would be married, but Hopkins' vow of poverty meant he had no present for this man who would recall well into the next century the exact moment in childhood when he looked up to see Gerard aloft, dizzy snatches of him among leaves—"very high," he said, in the garden's monstrous elm, too high, and no, he would not come down. Here, earthbound, years and miles away, Hopkins gathered up the feathers and sent them off, probably the oddest wedding gift of that dim bright day.

❦

Things seed and reseed. Five years later, in Wales, Hopkins would redream the dream in part. Ordained, and perhaps happier than he would be again, he let "The Windhover" fly from him, in fierce enjambment.

> I caught this morning's minion king-
> dom of daylight's dauphin, dapple-dawn-drawn Falcon, in
>   his riding
> Of the rolling level underneath him steady air, and
>   striding
> High there, how he rung upon the rein of a wimpling wing
> In his ecstasy! then off, off forth on swing,
>   As a skate's heel sweeps smooth on a bow-bend: the hurl
>   and gliding
>   Rebuffed the big wind. My heart in hiding
> Stirred for a bird,—the achieve of, the mastery of the
>   thing!

❦

How long does fascination take—a minute? a lifetime to be lifted out of self? Everything, of course, might begin with pleasure—Hopkins on canoeing, say, his first year at Oxford: "The motion is Elysian . . . a canoe in the Cherwell must be the summit of human happiness," he told his mother. So motion is poetic, one word triggering the next and the next. "When weeds, in wheels," Hopkins writes in "Spring," "shoot long and lovely and lush; / Thrush's eggs look little low heavens, and thrush / Through the echoing timber does so rinse and wring / The ear. . . ."

Wales helped, and reading Welsh, translating Welsh, the breathless tactics of its poets—the *cynghanedd*, the "consonant chime" that rushes noun on adjective, thinning verbs to barebone force, dropping articles and mere connectives for exclamations, declarations, to press the hidden nerve in words, those brother, sister twinning sounds. "Delightfully the bright wind boisterous ropes, wrestles, beats / earth bare / Of yestertempest's creases; in pool and rutpeel parches / Squandering ooze to squeezed dough, crust, dust; stanches, / starches / Squadroned masks and manmarks treadmire toil there / Footfretted in it."

This dates from his last, foul years at University College, Dublin, teaching Latin and Greek—so badly he thought—and all but broken by additional outside exams, some seven hundred essays five times a year to be gone over, graded. Years, he would write to Bridges, of a sorrow so great in him it "resembled madness." . . . *bright wind boisterous ropes, wrestles, beats / earth bare / of yestertempest's creases. . . .*

Can despair outlast such richness? Can ecstasy?

❧

"Stepped into . . . a great shadowy barn. . ." he wrote.

❧

1988, and here we've been weeks into the summer drought. I read that Hopkins prized Purcell's above all music. "Something necessary and eternal" he wrote, likening him to Milton for his friend, R. W. Dixon, although "none of your d—d subjective rot," he added, to Bridges. And I hear stories, perhaps apocryphal, of Hopkins going night after night, especially in those last hard years, to listen in the small, cramped concert rooms. I riffle through our records to find the Purcell, and lower the old complaining needle. The house is changed, charged, alight with news. Upstairs, my husband stops his hammering a moment. Strange swooping and gliding, shadowed by the ancient minor key. Press Hopkins there, and it is terrible, too haunting: ". . . only I'll / Have an eye to the sakes of him," Hopkins wrote in his poem about the man, "quaint moonmarks, to his / pelted plumage under / Wings. . . ."

🍃

Quaint moonmarks. "What must it be to be someone else?" Hopkins claimed to have asked in childhood, his thirst as intense as it was particular. Feeling, imagery, point, high thought, and flow of language were all well enough, he said to Coventry Patmore, in dismissing the young Yeats whom he met for all of ten minutes in 1886. The essential, the "only lasting thing" in poetry was *inscape*—a "species or individually distinctive beauty of style." Common speech, of course, drawing in through sound and image the ordinary moments of our lives, but engaged, enlarged by what is irreplaceable, personal, quirky: call it simply *surprise*, the cherished thing against a life of high order, a Jesuit life that Hopkins chose—more— rebelled into. "Glory be to God," the poem begins, not for the picturesque, predicted beauty, but with a curious, zoom-lens focus, for "dappled things—"

> For skies of couple-colour as a brinded cow;
>   For rose-moles all in stipple upon trout that swim;
> Fresh-firecoal chestnut-falls; finches' wings;
>   Landscape plotted and pieced—fold, fallow, and plough;
>   And all trades, their gear and tackle and trim.
>
> All things counter, original, spare, strange;
>   Whatever is fickle, freckled (who knows how?)
>   With swift, slow; sweet, sour; adazzle, dim
> He fathers-forth whose beauty is past change: Praise him.

How close are we to talk of Hopkins' "sprung rhythm" in this odd-angled point of view? "Sprung," Hopkins spelled out to Dixon, "means something like *abrupt.*" Something, we could say, exactly like that one loved thing in Purcell: "Not mood in him nor meaning, proud fire or sacred fear," Hopkins wrote,

"Or love or pity or all that sweet notes not his might nursle: /
It is the forged feature finds me; it is the rehearsal / Of own,
of abrupt self there so thrusts on, so throngs the ear."

❦

But gesture begets gesture. And for Hopkins, playful spin-
ning habit. This early journal entry begins, as usual, in the 3-
D world: "Drops of rain hanging on rails . . . lighted like nails
(of fingers)," then "Screws of brooks and twines." Then those
eerie "globes of cloud on a night with a moon faint or con-
cealed." All reasonable enough, but wait. "Blunt buds of the
ash," he adds. "Pencil buds of the beech. Lobes of the trees.
Cups of the eyes." We are quickening now, into deep associa-
tion. ". . . Bows of the eyelids. Pencil of eyelashes. Juices of
the eyeball. Eyelids like leaves, petals, caps, tufted hats, hand-
kerchiefs, sleeves, gloves . . . bones sleeved in flesh. Juices of
the sunrise." And then—our origin back, the final startling
of such a list—"Vermilion look of the hand held against a
candle," he writes, ". . . especially the knuckles covered with
ash."

Hopkins here was twenty-two, still at Oxford, eleven years
from the first of two great turns in his power coming in the
rash of poems—"The Windhover," "Pied Beauty," "God's
Grandeur," and others—that would break from him in Wales.
At this point, his poems were largely well-mannered versions
of what would go for family magazines, or school awards. But
here, in journal secrecy, the wellspring flashed and advanced
in dramatic build. "Bones sleeved in flesh . . . juices of the
sunrise," the hand lit—as if within—by candle, the knuckle,
our clue to final ash. *A rehearsal of own*, Hopkins wrote in
praise of Purcell, though he might well have praised himself,
even here, in practice.

❦

"I awoke in the Midsummer not-to-call night," he wrote in a
fragment years later, "in the white / and the walk of the

morning: / The moon, dwindled and thinned to the fringe of a fingernail / held to the candle. . . ."

❦

Perhaps it was genetic, this original nerve. First, say, the poet's father, Manley Hopkins, a quiet London marine-insurance adjuster, who, seized by all manner of raptures, would publish books of verse, a history of Hawaii, a handbook of averages still used in law schools, a study on the supernatural root of numbers. Or consider his Aunt Frances canoeing straight through the Canadian wilderness, whose watercolors of the *voyageurs* are still prized and displayed. "Why can't you be an ordinary Catholic," Hopkins' younger brother, Lionel, nagged the new Jesuit—Lionel, who himself would opt out of the predictable to pass much of his life in China, learning classical Chinese, translating the ancient incised bones.

Such habit incites stories: Hopkins, say, rushing out after any rain to witness the glittering path of crushed quartz that ran through the seminary gardens at Stonyhurst. "Ay, a strang yoong man, crouching down that gate to stare at some wet sand," recalled a lay brother years later. "A fair natural 'e seemed to us, that Mr. 'Opkins." By 1881, however, such things were endearing no longer, at least to Hopkins' own eye. "You give me a long jobation about eccentricities," he wrote in exhaustion to Bridges from his assistantship in a Liverpool parish. "Alas, I have heard so much and suffered so much for and in fact been so completely ruined for life by my alleged singularities that they are a sore subject."

❦

This many times before the wire knots, that many before it tangles and strains.

Hopkins' passion for the fourteenth-century Franciscan philosopher Duns Scotus worked against the Jesuit obsession with Aquinas and Aristotle, especially the poet's feeling for Scotus' notion of *haeccitas* or "thisness," an individual essence countering the older idea of matter as single, unsplintered.

"When I consider my selfbeing," he wrote in his 1880 commentary on Ignatius' *Exercises*, "that taste of myself, of *I* and *me* above and in all things . . . more distinctive than the taste of ale or alum, more distinctive than the smell of walnutleaf or camphor. . . . Nothing else in nature comes near this unspeakable stress of pitch. . . ." In 1872, finding Scotus' book tucked away in the library at Stonyhurst struck Hopkins as "a mercy from God." *Thisness*: a sudden eye in focus, a way to the miraculous thing. "But just then," he wrote later from the Isle of Man, "when I took in any inscape of the sky or sea I thought of Scotus." *All things counter, original, spare, strange*. In seminary, his Aristotelian examiners angered. Duns Scotus? An oddball, a dunce. It cost Hopkins for the rest of his life; in any case, his chance for an additional crowning year of study at Stonyhurst was dismissed, never mentioned.

More, it was muscle and nerve tightening in the coil of his own invention—sprung rhythm. Abrupt, as he said, his claim to the struck chord, the illuminating moment perfected in meter overstressed again and again by the ancient, alert spondee. No digression in such a rhythm, the choice is pure aim, no irony, no meandering into greater complication than strict, straightforward earnestness allows. All in natural service to the extreme gifts—a joy barely possible it is so great, a sorrow almost unspeakable. What must it be, growing conscious of more subtle forms, a widening of human thinking and circumstance, to find oneself, at midlife, still wedded, locked in by theory and habit to the young loved trance: only so high, so low a heaven, and nothing—none of one's day by plain day—between. No place for that in one's poems.

But his trouble was Whitman too—Hopkins' on-again, off-again attraction. "I may as well say what I should not otherwise have said," he admitted unhappily to Bridges in 1882, "that I always knew in my heart Walt Whitman's mind to be more like my own than any other man's living. And as he is a very great scoundrel," he added, "this is not a pleasant confession." One turns immediately to Emily Dickinson, that other American counterpart, Hopkins' equal or better in her elliptical brilliance. Her remark on Whitman was chilling: "I never read his book—but was told he was disgraceful." Unlike her,

Hopkins allowed himself such dangers, though only in doses, and not many at that. ". . . the more desirous (I am) to read him . . . the more determined . . . I will not," he finally promised Bridges.

❧

Whitman's famous reverie continued on toward the end of the century. "I believe a leaf of grass is no less than the journeywork of the stars," he wrote, "And the running blackberry would adorn the parlors of heaven, / And the narrowest hinge in my hand puts to scorn all machinery. . . ." See the hand, then, opening, closing on itself, the hand abruptly ghosted— luminous—over something close to Hopkins' candle. Ecstasy's peril is its timing, high and quick. Journeywork, Whitman said, *running* blackberry, a hinge real or imagined in the hand's bone certainty—these fly past, and leave behind their arguments. Brother to Whitman, Hopkins could write in the present tense both of them cherished this river scene, its children aloft, on ropes: " . . . how the boys / With dare and with downdolphinry and bellbright bodies / huddling out, / Are earthworld, airworld, waterworld thorough hurled, all by / turn and turn about." A moment, like Whitman's, right now, immediate. But this piece is from a fragment; the poet quit it and would not go back.

❧

So the trees slow this summer, phantom collapse in the drought, mimicking fall with their yellow leaves. I read the paper, the good botanist who says simply how the trees will live regardless. But of course they are wounded, he says. Not next year, but the next will tell, or the next, or the next. They are that much closer to disease, weakened by these nights that never cool down. The sun won't blink. I imagine the dark rings in the heart of each tree, the thin sullen orbit that will be this summer: nothing to add, just hanging on.

❧

Thus a life veers off, declines, diminishes. One cuts, picks another thread to follow down for treasure, believing that treasure waits. Almost nothing Hopkins wrote was published in his lifetime, but so much fretted over, dreamt and redreamt. How many do we count? The book on Greek meter—never finished. "St. Winefred's Well," a verse drama—left. His study of harmony, and actual music, songs and canons; his account of light and ether—both barely past their outlines. A book on Egyptian art—half researched. A study of Aeschylus and Homer, and St. Patrick's confession, a critical edition—only half envisioned. All heaped, a pile of shards. Fragment after fragment of poetry beneath that, like layers of cities, ancient and airless and pinned senseless below our word *city*. Add the journal, everything to its last fitful line, broken off violently, midsentence, in 1875. Some lost things are simply lost. These are easy, our worry. But the inner shattered thing was Hopkins' own: ". . . all my world is scaffolding," he wrote bitterly to Bridges, those last years. "All impulse fails me. . . ."

❧

All impulse but the darkest sort. "O the mind, mind has mountains," he wrote in 1885, "cliffs of fall / Frightful, sheer, no-man fathomed. Hold them cheap / May who ne'er hung there." If we could follow Ignatius' keen-eyed method, and vanish into that most spiritual of exercises, what would we see of the man who wrote this? What, image by image, could we call out of nowhere?

A line of winter trees, first, along Dublin's St. Stephen's Green, back and up to a window there, then the real desk in focus, a straight-backed chair, a man whose eyes are "hazel" almost brown, though "slightly darker at the outer rims." And further, in ghostly X-ray, "heart and vitals, all shaggy with the whitest hair." But these are Hopkins' words. He's writing, pinned in lamplight. It's early evening, nasty weather, too cold and wet, too much work ahead. We might stand there in the doorway transfixed as he is, not embarrassed.

❧

Perhaps sorrow enters the body through the gregarious mind, smuggled in with all bright landscapes, held there in every given gorgeous detail. But it's the body that first grasps the ticking course. Pretty virus, we might say, this sadness, its microscopic beauty slow and almost winning, but years show themselves years, joy ground down to something else. Inevitable, perhaps, for Hopkins. You think Stevenson's Hyde is overdrawn, he pressed Bridges. "My Hyde is worse." In a few months, by 1887, such revelation was second nature. These "hard wearing wasting wasted years," he wrote. But no one's ever matched his wonder; and no despondency has been so brilliant. "I wake and feel the fell of dark, not day," he wrote early in those Dublin years.

> What hours, O what black hours we have spent
> This night! what sights you, heart, saw; ways you went!
> And more must, in yet longer light's delay.
>   With witness I speak this. But where I say
> Hours I mean years, mean life. And my lament
> Is cries countless, cries like dead letters sent
> To dearest him that lives alas! away.

>   I am gall, I am heartburn. God's most deep decree
> Bitter would have me taste: my taste was me;
> Bones built in me, flesh filled, blood brimmed the curse.
>   Selfyeast of spirit a dull dough sours. I see
> The lost are like this, and their scourge to be
> As I am mine, their sweating selves; but worse.

❦

Despair. Its wire thickens to re-create, quiets. A kind of antiseptic, never local. It abstracts itself. It doesn't break.

❦

Such witness. Drop down years through it, following back the journals to Stonyhurst, this clue: late spring 1873, and Hopkins is not yet twenty-nine, working in another of so many rooms. "The ashtree growing in the corner of the garden was felled," he begins, too calmly. "It was lopped first: I heard the sound and looking out and seeing it maimed there came at that moment a great pang. . . ." We can pause here as he did not. In this no less violent year, I hear my own outside. Cars in their tiny lives go by; men keep drilling, pounding, tearing up the street.

Thirst and Patience

Her thirst, perhaps, began in childhood, and patience too, passionate as seed. After all, getting there was an equal gift, crossing to the island—Monhegan Island, Maine—those summers that slowly turned as the last century geared down, disappeared into this one, and the island, ten miles off shore, kept its own beauty sleepily. The idea came from her mother—Mary Warner Moore—for whatever reason: to get her children, Warner and Marianne, out of the heat of Carlisle, Pennsylvania; to witness herself—landlocked, Missouri bred, her husband lost, institutionalized—what was coolly, lushly visible. Here was the island's sweating, raw board ice house, and the pond beside it, cut and harvested every winter since 1874, going nearly lagoon in summer, languid, dizzy with birds. Here was Lobster Cove, wet and dangerous ("No one has ever been saved who fell overboard or from rocks here," the village pamphlets warn), and the woods beyond, solemn with pine. Enough for children, certainly. Enough finally to make Mary Warner Moore come close to building a house here, settling permanently. Later, in 1933, Marianne Moore would recall those days when she and her mother reached the island by a sailboat called *The Effort*, arriving at low tide, which is to say, midnight, hobbling "over stones . . . by lantern-light" to the "gabled attic room in a fisherman's cottage." Now crossing eighty, ninety years beyond those summers, it is enough to put such reverie against the chill sea air. And there, eider ducks in stiff flying formation, and seals on sudden outcroppings of rock, stilled by sun. Our boat takes its long hour to get there, progressing, as Marianne Moore wrote of such boats, "white and rigid as if in / a grove."

Impossible, finally, to judge the weight of such memory, this island of folktale austerity, but we have some evidence. There it is, Moore admitted, in "The Steeple-Jack," the piece that opens her *Complete Poems* with clear color ("a sea the purple of the peacock's neck"), and a wonder that recognizes waves "as formal as the scales / on a fish," or the ornate "sugar bowl shaped summer house" liked because the source of such elegance "is not bravado." Like Ambrose, the student she invents for the poem, we see the town Durer would have embraced for its fine complexity: "eight stranded whales to look at," or aloft, the gulls who sail about the lighthouse "without moving their wings." These scenes offer themselves in painterly ways. But such beauty is surprisingly barbed. Or so her poem proves, narrowing down to an ominous heart. "Danger," the sign in red and white declares at the church whose spire the steeple jack climbs, danger against the spire's "Solid- / pointed star, which . . . / stands for hope." As in good painting, in good poems one waits for the final click. *Danger*. The thing unnerves. Its tension, its ticking, is mystery.

It was John Ruskin who turned this instinct into iron, handing down with deliberate passion three laws in his *Elements of Drawing*—unity, individuality, mystery—the last asserting that "nothing is ever seen perfectly, but only by fragments," a thought that slips quickly, lyrically, into more personal matters. "How little," he adds, "we may hope to discern clearly, to judge justly, the rents and veins of the human heart." Nature was lesson, moral lesson. To see was to think and to discover, for Ruskin and probably for Moore who read and valued him, referring to him in years of essays. In everything shone this hard, unknowable thing—mystery, danger—a careful, clear-eyed attention the only option.

It is no accident, then, that "The Steeple-Jack" moves with such visual intelligence though early or late, painting and drawing were habit most of Moore's life, an obsession beyond the commonplace books and daybooks fashionable among educated women at the turn of the century. Her need was established in high school, and though by college she had dropped her own professional ambitions in painting, there were hundreds of drawings ahead of her, thousands of hours over many years. What was at stake? "You must add yourself to what you see, and infuse the object with the passionate essence of your own thought," her good friend, sculptor Malvina Hoffman wrote, ". . . the result will be the merging of matter and spirit."

The idea was not Ruskin's, but Rodin's. Hoffman came under his influence early, at twenty-five, leaving New York for Paris with the feverish resolve of studying with the master. At seventy, deluged with admirers, awards and commissions, finally certain of his reputation, Rodin was a difficult man to meet. She came armed with photographs of two heads she had sculpted; her father's, pianist Richard Hoffman, and that of the young violinist Samuel Crimson, whom she would marry fourteen years later, in 1924. This was the story Moore herself loved to tell: how her friend, after five attempts, was finally admitted to the Rue d'Université studio; how going off to lunch, Rodin had locked her in so she could study his work in solitude; how on his return, the fire out in the large damp room, he had wrapped his cloak around her, lecturing her furiously about health. Hoffman stayed on for months. She held her experience there above any in her life. At a time when many artists were rethinking the whole business of form, pressed by the excitement of impressionism, cubism, and other abstractions, it was Rodin who kept high his old passion. "Do not be afraid of realism," she quoted him as saying. "To understand nature is a lifelong study." Marianne Moore, two years younger than Hoffman, had just been graduated from Bryn Mawr, and was enrolled in Carlisle Commercial College to study a whole set of equally realistic, if unnatural, things— typing, shorthand, bookkeeping—subjects she would teach beginning in the fall of 1911 at the U.S. Industrial Indian School in Carlisle. That summer, though, she and her mother froze everything and went to Europe, Moore keeping scrupulous visual accounts of what she saw, beginning what would be a lifetime of sketchbooks. These early collections held a rich summary: window seats, men in hats, gothic doorways, garden walks, fishes, ships, faces, birds. "Art is contemplation," Rodin had said. Which is to say, it is heightened observation, paying attention; it is time.

Time. "Slowness makes it large," Moore wrote years later in one of her sketchbooks, "& swiftness weak." On the opposite page, dated Nov. 6, 1943, she had placed a large red leaf over the drawing of that leaf, deeply veined, its shades rendered by colored pencil. There, the thing itself, and below it what the mind makes of it, what muscle and time make. One might revolve a long time before this mystery: the actual leaf, brittle now, wholly *past*; the drawing still in the alert ready passage we call present. Is it possible to imagine this? Moore secreting the leaf from whatever garden, placing it here, so amazed at its intricacy that she wished to know it through eye and hand, and in doing so, perhaps forget—what? news of war, or the neighborhood of trees going empty into winter, or whatever human daily tedium fills the brain to numbness? Contemplation, or as her friend Malvina Hoffman put it, this "merging of matter and spirit," was at the heart of the method, for poet, for artist.

The two women, however, did not meet until 1949, although Moore knew of Hoffman's work, and even wrote of it with a backhanded praise in a piece on the dancer Anna Pavlova done for *The Nation* in 1945. They finally spoke when both became members of the Academy of Arts and Letters, meeting often for supper in the artist's Manhattan studio. "After an evening of talk," Hoffman wrote, "I would put her in a cab to return her to her Brooklyn home, arguing with the cabdriver who would usually protest against going to that faraway place." Hoffman claimed to understand few of Moore's poems. "She didn't mind my saying what I did," the artist wrote, "she liked the truth, a mending kind of adhesive. . . ." Hoffman was more useful to Moore when the poet began her translations of La Fontaine's *Fables*—a little more useful, anyway. "She would call me up on the phone late at night and ask me to do an unrehearsed, direct translation for her . . . then she would read me (hers) . . . I would say 'Is that the same fable?' for her translation would be full of adjuncts and additions and curious new angles and light. But without replying to me, she would ring off and go back to work."

What Hoffman could do—and did—was guide and encourage Moore's drawing and painting. For several summers, they spent weeks at a time on the Maine coast, busy, as Hoffman put it, with "our usual undramatic tasks": painting, taking drives, reading, writing. In 1955, they stayed a few weeks in Louis Hyde's summer place in Kittery, an old sea captain's house, formerly owned by F. O. Matthiessen. Their daily outings were simple: a couple of afternoon hours at the dock or in the woods, doing watercolors. "We would go, for example, to a granite quarry . . . to me, a very exciting place . . .—all pinks and grays," Hoffman wrote. "I'd be trying to get all of it at once, as usual, the three floors of ladders going down to the water below, the derricks, the men working. But Marianne would select just one thing, a piece of chain on a pulley, and paint that." Her work, Hoffman admitted, was "perfectly evocative and imaginative," a comment hard to interpret. Moore's own version of her efforts was typically modest. ". . . I could not get the chimney realistic. Miss Hoffman corrected my angles, and after supper demonstrated for me the axiomatically interacting principles of perspective." The painting she speaks of—a watercolor of Matthiessen's house—is one of Moore's most detailed, elegant pieces, the only painting of her own she allowed to be hung in her living room.

Hoffman's description of Moore's habit—zeroing in on one element of a scene and painting *that*—is characteristic of her approach to poems as well. It's true that she is careful in "The Steeple-Jack" to give us first a wide-angled feel for place, but the eye is drawn quickly into the real heat of the poem: the danger sign against the church's calm. One suspects it is this image in its matter-of-fact perversity that initially caught the poet and induced her onward into the piece. In "A Grave," a more urgently philosophical poem, the play of concrete elements takes us breathlessly into more abstract reverie quite from the beginning. About the sea, "it is human nature to stand in the middle of a thing, / but you cannot stand in the middle of this; / the sea has nothing to give but a well-excavated grave. . . ." Whatever the outcome of Moore's contemplation here, the poem's "literal origin," as Moore wrote of it, was again a single focus: Monhegan Island once more, where "a man . . . placed himself between my mother and me, and the surf we were watching from a middle ledge of rocks . . . 'Don't be annoyed,'" Moore remembers her mother remarking, "'It is human nature to stand in the middle of a thing.'"

Moore's stance throughout many of her poems, her fascination for things both human made and natural, does not have the immediate physical freshness of, say, William Carlos Williams, who in his observant "Spring and All" offers the roadside world with colloquial flash and grace, (". . . the reddish, / purplish, forked, upstanding, twiggy / stuff of bushes and small trees.") Moore, instead, notices things—as in her well-known poem "The Fish"—with the savor of someone who has come like a painter on a quest to look at things, and little else. "The fish / wade / through black jade. / If the crow blue mussel shells, one keeps / adjusting the ash-heaps; / opening and shutting like a / injured fan." There is lush gravity in such description that makes clear why Louise Bogan would complain to her friend Morton Zabel, that though she, Bogan, wanted to write about "things naturally elegant, like pineapples and shells and feathers," she could not. "M. Moore," she went on, "has rather a lien on objects characterized by natural elegance, hasn't she? I'd have to be very lyrical about them, in order to get them out of her class; the class that presents and imaginatively constructs and describes. . . ."

That class, I suppose, could rightly be called "imagist," those drawn to Pound's idea of image as presenting "an intellectual and emotional complex in an instant of time," but Moore refused the title, claiming simply that she liked to describe things, the emphasis squarely on process. Several times in her essays she remarks that our chance of happiness is greater if we want to *do* something rather than *have* something. Given this, one might wonder why the poet herself seemed intent on keeping everything, a zealous pack rat filling up notebook after notebook with clippings and letters, even her books serving as file cabinets, some swollen three times their size. Now lovingly reassembled at Philadelphia's Rosenbach Museum, her famous living room is a place, no, a world, nearly overcome in mementoes—animal knickknacks, paintings, baseballs—so much stately, whimsical clutter, the bulk of which, it seems fair to add, was given to her over years by friends. "No ideas but in things" might seem a fit, if predictable, caption. Not things particularly beautiful in themselves, but exactly so because they *refer*—the blue ceramic camel given to her by E. E. Cummings, or the Ojibway quill box with a dollar bill and a note from her brother inside, or even the baseball signed by Mickey Mantle and Joe Dimaggio. Her things narrow and activate the power of a life lived. "My idea of research," she told Grace Schulman in one of her last interviews, "(is to) look at a thing from all sides." A looking, no doubt, that she managed as painter or poet, exacting—as she said of other people's art in her poem "When I Buy Pictures"—"the spiritual forces which have made it," this thing inside "lit with piercing glances into the life of things."

This, perhaps, is one definition of patience, reliable as lunch, this part of Moore that Bogan celebrated in the *Quarterly Review of Literature*'s special issue on Moore in 1948 as the "moralist (though a gentle one) . . . a stern—though flexible—technician." But most astonishing about Moore's work, both poems and drawings, is its immense quirkiness *anyway*, an exuberance that Bogan has called "high Rococo." As for Moore, the method is only sideways admitted. "There is something attractive about a mind that moves in a straight line—" she writes in rich amusement, in her poem "People's Surroundings"—

> the municipal bat-roost of mosquito warfare;
> the American string quartet;
> these are questions more than answers,
>
> and Bluebeard's Tower above the coral-reefs,
> the magic mouse-trap closing on all points of the compass,
> capping like petrified surf the furious azure of the bay,
> where there is no dust, and life is like a lemon-leaf,
> a green piece of tough translucent parchment,
> where the crimson, the copper, and Chinese vermillion of
>   the poincianas
> set fire to the masonry and turquoise blues refute the
>   clock . . .
>
> and the acacia-like lady shivering at the touch of a hand,
> lost in a small collision of the orchids. . . .

As tough and detailed as this writing is, its movement and color are a drug. We forget everything, almost, in its intricate incantation.

Moore's drawings—some—radiate an equal light. Once inside the Rosenbach Museum where the poet left everything behind, one participates in ritual. Visitors strip down to pencil and notebook. One sits at the high monastery table and pulls from the storage box a blue serge sketchbook. There, page 1, placed in the spine are two small airy feathers—*feathers*, bluish, gray—and the date, in pencil: June 1916. Then see this— a single claw foot, expertly drawn, raised as if in horror or flight, midpage, alone. In 1916, Moore was twenty-nine. Her first poems had appeared in the *Egoist, Poetry*, and *Others*. She and her mother, "two chameleons," she said, had just moved to Chatham, New Jersey, to keep house in her brother's parsonage. These are facts. But this—these feathers, this page out of a young woman's notebook—is intense imagination. Not the public solitude of her watercolors where one feels hours spent gazing down a dark-leafed road in woods, or near the lobster pilings where water can be seen through the windows of the sagging fishing shack. The solitude of this claw is not so picturesque, not generalized by beauty. In the process of composition, in the drawing itself, something has happened, some interior resistance is defined.

Curiosity defined. Some might say eccentricity defined. "I like county fairs," she wrote in 1951 at sixty-four, "roller coasters . . . dog shows, experiments in timing like our ex-Museum of Science and Invention's two roller-bearings in a gravity chute. I . . . take an inordinate interest in mongooses, squirrels, crows, elephants." What, in fact, pleased her about her friends might have been a similar quirk of mind. In her piece on Malvina Hoffman, she praises the artist's tool case, which included a "Javanese dagger ending in a bird—its strong angled claws grasping a snake—the bird's circular white eyes staring down on the upturned circular white eyes of the snake. . . ." The snake and the bird, their resolution and terror frozen thus propelling the blade: the *idea* of knife in its grand cruel purpose. "A very emotional object," she adds, stepping back. Yet the same woman could spend what must have been a long time drawing a live tarantula in 1932. It fills the whole page of a serge notebook with poisonous immediacy, undercut by its no-nonsense caption. "The common name of this large spider is properly accented on the second syllable—tarantula. Putting the accent on the third syllables not correct." Louise Bogan might have sensed the "stern, flexible technician" in such a remark, and certainly a great deal of Moore's drawing has deliberate intention. She was fond, she said, of museums, and notebook after notebook delivers this affection. One sees her rigid before the long glass cases, at work in one of her favorite places, New York's Natural History Museum, rendering silk moths, or a portable brass compass. One imagines her drawing quickly, deftly, a Manchurian pheasant at the Armory's Poultry Show in the late 1930s, or copying intricate tile designs at the Iranian Institute. But this too is curiosity defined, a hospitality toward the daily treasure that bombards us. Or perhaps will has little to do with it. "People ask me," Moore said in 1967 (though she might well have been asked about her drawing), "How do you think of things to write about? I don't. They think of me. They become irresistible."

This might be a puzzling kind of ambition that waits for things to declare themselves, but desire is often alerted by patience. And thirst—much of its power must be surprise. In answer, one watercolor is revealing: a young woman caught up not in herself, but in her work, poised over it, her back to us, her concentration a visible power. Part of that patience, too, might have made Moore relaxed enough for whimsy—drawings of frogs speaking their nonsense, or later, red plums in cool gallop across the double page—or for a much different sort of ambition. Dead serious, Moore holds up an "Egyptian Pulled Glass Bottle in the Shape of a Fish," and says with absolute clarity:

> Here we have thirst
> and patience; from the first,
> and art, as in a wave held up for us to see
> in its essential perpendicularity:
>
> not brittle, but
> intense—the spectrum, that

spectacular and nimble animal the fish,
whose scales turn aside the sun's sword by their polish.

How something comes into being is a miracle of the first
order. We call it coherence, or more glibly, form. I don't imag-
ine Moore ever got over the gift of its presence, or thought for
a moment it was easy, this "violence within," as she said, quot-
ing Wallace Stevens, "that protects us from a violence with-
out." Of course in her humility she refused to call her poems
Poems, but instead "exercises in composition," herself an "inter-
ested hack, rather than an author." Inarguable crimes for her
were snobbery, murkiness, intolerance. "Blessed the geniuses
who know / that egomania is not a duty," she wrote in her
poem "Blessed is the Man." Her own drawings and poems she
called her "kitchenware," scorning the piety with which so
many artists and writers talk about their work. She spoke little
of hers, preferring, in interviews and essays, to address the
world: baseball, Indian sign language, the history and aesthet-
ics of knives, the work of her contemporaries. For that *QRL*
special issue, her friend, Elizabeth Bishop, called her, without
hyperbole, "The World's Greatest Living Observer," praising
her eye. And earlier, in a letter quoted by Lynn Keller—"I
don't know how without seeing Key West you managed to do
it, but what you said about its being a 'kind of ten command-
ments of vegetable dye printing' is the best description yet."
Such skill, though, should not be too surprising for a poet
whose lifelong apprenticeship lay with line and color, pencil
and brush. So she astounds us, as William Carlos Williams
wrote in that same issue, by setting us to look "at some appar-
ently small object," and in it feel "the swirl of great events."
Humility might not absolutely evoke brilliance in poetry or
anything else, but it does provide perspective, the crucial abil-
ity to forget, momentarily anyway, one's true place as center
of the universe, and so usher in, *see*, perhaps even transfer
into art, the world's real wealth.

Thus one imagines Moore's stubborn choice of Brooklyn
over Manhattan, this place, wrote Marguerite Young about an
afternoon visit with the poet "so generally depicted as the
arid jumping off place," or at best a strange "mixture of the

archaic and the modern," the latter description not altogether unsuitable for Moore herself. Her street—Cumberland—was Whitman's too, however briefly, in 1852. It is, of course, still there; her lovely old apartment house as well whose three stone lions gaze about the entry way in blank rapture. Here Moore lived for thirty-six years, watching a scarlet tanager take root in a nearby white magnolia, walking to the zoo and the Botanic Gardens, taking in so many lectures at the Brooklyn Institute of Arts and Sciences, that she was "pitied at home for not being able to sleep in the building." Down the block, her corner grocery continues, and Fort Greene Park still waits at the street's other end where the old revolutionary fort stood.

It was New Year's Day when I made my pilgrimage. The exterior door was broken but still wrought iron, still banked by a stone cornucopia of fruits and vegetables on either side: apples and squash and grapes, over-ripened, splitting open to seed. I began, as Moore might have, to draw, though unlike her, I wanted everything in my sketchbook—the lions, of course, but even the sticker plastered on the inner marble wainscoting, its Cheshire cat gleaming above the Day-Glo letters: *I luv your smile*, even the bright message, *I was hear*, spray painted on the outer wall. Two doors down, the little Mount Carmel Church of God In Christ, Inc. was silent; no one, in fact, was on the street. My mother-in-law waited, reading in the car, until I climbed back in, and we started for Manhattan, over Brooklyn Bridge, which Moore loved as much as any poet has, and into the Village. It was there I noticed that my favorite gray beret had vanished. We stopped the car, and searched. Nothing. "Maybe it fell out when you got out in Brooklyn," my mother-in-law said. Then, weakly: "Do you want to go back?" "It won't be there," I said, "this is New York." But we did drive back, the traffic thickened now, the winter afternoon graying, almost silver.

She parked at the corner, and took up her book again. I ran down Cumberland Street, breathless, past two young cops chatting, twirling their nightsticks. Half a block away, an old man pulled his good wicker green shopping cart, the kind my grandmother believed in too. I stopped suddenly right there, thinking: this is the place she chose, this is the place she knew by heart. Now the building—five stories high with its somber lions—was startlingly hers. I could see its elegance up ahead, inscrutable in that broken street, and solid. "I tend to like a poem," the poet wrote, "which instead of culminating in a crescendo, merely comes to a close." And an essay too, I imagine. So for you, Miss Moore, thank you. My hat was still there.

Plath's Bees

Nearly thirty years to the month, the days had turned unexpectedly warm. October—a word so rough and rich to say—stood ancient, and brilliant as usual, if any sort of genius is usual. A friend of a friend had promised to show me bees; now was the time. The odd summerlike temperatures had roused and gentled them, he said as we turned off Route 26 into woods, the quiet its own sudden creature.

I had imagined a winding road—there it was—and of course a meadow. Then a ring of grub maple and tulip trees, and because we weren't far from the river, two great, sad sycamores. These were the university's bees. I had wanted to see a home site, something closer to Sylvia Plath's own venture in Devon where she kept one colony through its first real season, the summer of 1962, before her death the following winter. But my companion said this was exactly *like* such a place, more so than his own backyard where trees had gradually, over twenty years, encroached on the hives to cast them into shade that made them cross, easily angered. We stopped, and I saw the hives: nine gleaming layered boxes set evenly apart in the clearing's wild grass, cool and restful and weird. They seemed to hover there, the trees behind them just turning—red, and a yellow almost blinding.

October still, and almost thirty years before Plath crossed through this stillness and wrote her bee sequence, five poems, in one sleepless week. Say the words: bee box, pupa, pollen, venom. The busy dark interior I had yet to see. I had been warned to wear light colors. It calmed the bees, my companion told me over the phone. If you wear white, he said, to them you're almost invisible.

❦

To be invisible. To be observer. "How shall I describe it?—" Plath wrote that last year about poetry itself, "a door opens, a door shuts. In between you have had a glimpse: a garden, a person, a rainstorm, a dragonfly, a heart, a city . . . So a poem takes place." But nothing is as brief or as happenstance, nothing so unasked for. It starts stubbornly in the body, and beyond—father and mother, even back of that. Which is to say, it starts in memory; we want to repeat. "What do I remember / that was shaped / as this thing is shaped?" Williams keeps insisting in "Asphodel, That Greeny Flower." A door opens and shuts, a glimpse. And it begins—the long unfolding into image, specific image culled from a life, two lives or more. Faced without sentiment or nostalgia, such images *release*. Coming first those last months, Plath's bee sequence did this; in its fierce incandescence, twenty-two other poems followed, and *Ariel* began to burn and take form.

The bees, of course, seemed to be waiting for Plath, arriving a full generation earlier. A coincidence, maybe a dark luck, but first there was a boy with a taste for honey almost a century ago in Germany, in the Polish corridor. And this boy, Otto Plath, filched a glass straw from the kitchen, wandered through fields and woods to find the underground bumblebee nests, carefully lowered his straw and—two to one— struck the cool secret in spite of the bees' fury. Soon he was keeping bees carried home gingerly in cigar boxes, set up in the garden. At this distance, the boy becomes a tiny romantic figure on the horizon, the *Bienenkonig*—the bee king—his childhood friends called him, half jeering. Still, he is at it, bent forward in the grass, alert for a sign.

All this equals; it is a cycle we will see in the daughter: solitude and danger, a palpable reward. *Ariel* in general and the bee poems in particular carry—are carried by—this electric pulse and focus. It's in the relentless questions that push the poems forward; it's the repeated words, phrases, whole lines, which, like a narrowing to the sexual instant or like some frenzied mantra, slow the narrative press while speeding up every lyric mystery beneath. Her repetitions break through time, give glimpse of a stranger place—"sweetness, sweetness" the poet nearly singsongs, painting the hive to call to the bees by color, or chanting "she is old, old, old," deepening the pitch, making the queen bee primal, a *first thing*, of myth.

But it isn't myth, not completely. The bee poems aren't all lost to trance and sadness, though these tempt us with their poison and splendor. Ordinary cause and effect is here, the bit by bit of things. Plath's brilliance is that balance. Certainly loss and rage, and a calm that might well be madness, but it's the bees we understand, the sound of them in a box or, come fall, the dark of the cellar with its silent honey jars. How far away now is the boy who stands listening in the grass for what might be hidden underground? Not science or art, not yet. This watchfulness is habit; he is merely curious.

❧

Simple tools for such a habit: I dutifully submitted to the veil, the gloves, part of the "moonsuit," Plath called it. But it was the smoker I loved. Half bellows, half oil can, something out of Dickens in its epic but domestic no-nonsense feel, the smoker is exactly that: it smokes. And as we moved toward the bees and opened the first hive, my companion puffed into it small rapid clouds from the smoldering wood chips in the firepot.

Instantly the bees, furious at our invasion, calmed into slow drunkenness, flew away or back to the combs to anchor themselves against the pollen or honey cells. The smoke, my companion told me, excites then subdues them. They give up the notion *predator*; the issue is larger, more catastrophic—a fire near the hive, it's pointless to fight. Instead they take off, or begin to gorge themselves with honey in preparation for flight.

But don't they know we're doing this, just the same? I

asked, helping him lift off the next heavy wooden layer—he called it a super—so we could see the combs up close. We're just the jiggling to them, he said. We're just what happens when the supers are moved. It's not in their code of responses to figure us out. But the smoke, it's older than we are; they know what to do with that.

I thought of our own codes locked in the brain, buried in cells, a prehistoric riddle. In college, I had a friend who knew all the things the mind refused to do; she had a list from class. One of them was picturing one's own body from a distance. Imagine you're sleeping, she liked to say. Now look down at yourself from the ceiling. But I couldn't. I got everything else in the dorm room right: the cinderblock walls, the pale linoleum. But when I approached the bed, the sense of myself sleeping there, the whole scene grayed out, a quick dissolve. I opened my eyes, then closed them, kept trying until it scared me to try.

Now in the open air, it was the wheeze of the bellows, the swirling dazzle of smoke and the sharp smell of it, the ominous buzzing suddenly lowered in volume and pitch. We were not ourselves but an element—a kind of charm to the bees in our perfect fraud.

❦

I looked down into the hive and saw what Plath saw. "The men were lifting out rectangular yellow slides, crusted with bees, crawling, swarming. . . ." This from the journal account of her first "bee-meeting," what Ted Hughes calls the "loose prose draft" toward her poem of the same name, the beginning of her famous sequence. "If a poem is concentrated, a closed fist," Plath wrote, "then a novel is relaxed, and expansive, an open hand. . . . Where the first excludes and stuns, the open hand can touch and encompass a great deal in its travels."

Plath's journal piece is just such an open hand, distinctive in its wit and description, its fine shifts of tone: an *English* beekeeping meeting, with all the quirky village findings of a Barbara Pym. Before us is the rector, his headgear a dark

affair with a screened box attached ("I thought the hat a cleri-
cal beekeeping hat," Plath tells us), then the midwife and her
"moony beam," and one of the local dowagers "cadaverous as
a librarian." Throughout, the poet is alert to all the polite
conversation in orbit around Charlie Pollard—his are the bees
everyone's come to see—though gradually it is loosened by
the oddity of the gathering and the donning of its costumes.

"See all the bees round the rector's dark trousers," whispered
the woman. "They don't seem to like white." I was grateful for
my white smock. The rector was somehow an odd man out,
referred to now and then by Charlie jestingly: "Eh, rector?"
"Maybe they want to join his church," one man, emboldened
by the anonymity of the hats, suggested.

All this is drawn with sense, even affection, and with the
complexity that humor often supplies, but because this isn't
Barbara Pym but Sylvia Plath, the inevitable darkness and
weight enter. "The men were lifting slides," she writes:

Charlie Pollard squirting smoke into another box. They were
looking for queen cells—long, pendulous honey colored cells
from which the new queens would come. The blue-coated
woman pointed them out. She was from British Guiana, had
lived alone in the jungle for eighteen years, lost 25 pounds on
her first bees there—there was no honey for them to eat. I was
aware of bees buzzing and stalling before my face. The veil
seemed hallucinatory. I could not see it for moments at a time.
Then I became aware I was in a bone-stiff trance, intolerably
tense, and shifted round to where I could see better. "Spirit of
my dead father, protect me!" I arrogantly prayed. A dark,
rather nice, unruly-looking man came up through the cut
grass. Everyone turned, murmured "O Mr. Jenner, we didn't
think you were coming. . . ."

In her lightning shifts—from description and fact, through
the solitary near hallucination, to the distraction and camara-
derie of the group welcoming one of its members—we have
not only the authentic flash of thought, we have the *lens*
through which the poem will move out of the prose. Not the
sweet welcoming, that lens, nor even the smoky quest for the

queen. The bee sequence is launched in that moment of personal stillness: the bees stalling outside the veil, the slow alarm of that "bone-stiff trance," two lifetimes—father and daughter—in the desperate, affirmative prayer. So the open hand closes to the fist Plath speaks of. "I could not run without having to run forever," she admits halfway through her poem about that meeting.

> The white hive is snug as a virgin,
> Sealing off her brood cells, her honey, and quietly
>   humming.
>
> Smoke rolls and scarves in the grove.
> The mind of the hive thinks this is the end of everything.
>
> Here they come, the outriders, on their hysterical elastics.
> If I stand very still, they will think I am cow-parsley,
> A gullible head untouched by their animosity,
> Not even nodding, a personage in a hedgerow.
> The villagers open the chambers, they are hunting the queen.
> Is she hiding, is she eating honey? She is very clever.
> She is old, old, old, she must live another year, and
>   she knows it. . . .

A poem, Plath insisted, "excludes and stuns." And the precise strangeness of the imagery here—the hive "quietly humming," the bees' confused flight as "hysterical elastics," later, in the final stanza, the mob of them rising as "a blackout of knives"—does stun. The significance of this passage can be understood if by *excludes* she means that our witness has ruined us, at least briefly, for polite conversation, that we are outside, abruptly hypnotized by beauty that, as Rilke put it, is terror, or rather that part of terror that we can—but barely—endure.

❦

Poetry like Sylvia Plath's is not *good doggy* work; it neither behaves nor comforts. One doesn't like it in any usual affectionate sense of that word, but that's only the beginning of its power. The winnowing pressure that takes the bee meeting's prose version to its poetic form strikes me as careful and fevered as her father's writing in his book, *Bumblebees and Their Ways*, published when his daughter was two years old, in 1934, when he was teaching at Boston University.

As a collection of straight fact on bees, Otto Plath's effort is a failure. It reads differently than most modern treatises, which is to say, it *thinks* differently. The book doesn't conclude as much as it lets us bear witness. Otto Plath's old childhood habit, a restless, very physical research, is here. The winter digging by icepike, whole hives sometimes, that close attention to flight patterns and defensive postures, those endless returns to the sites to note every season's effect on the colonies: these are the things that matter. The book reads, in short, as field notes, with modesty and containment and absolute purpose. Still we are never far from that boy with nerve enough to lower his straw down to the underground nests; one is startled, again, by his fearlessness.

Example: Otto Plath writes at length about the bumblebee's defense of her nest. Either queen or worker will raise her legs in threatening ways, sometimes showing her stinger's droplet of venom. Not infrequently, she will shoot a stream of liquid at the intruder. He quotes an authority, one "Huber (1802)," insisting it is venom that is expelled, that "it does no harm, unless preceded by a perforation."

"In order to determine whether Huber's assertion is correct," Plath continues, "I pricked my finger with a pin and rubbed the liquid which had been ejected by an irritated worker of *B. terricola* into the wound but found it did not cause any pain. It is evident, therefore," he writes with a mild flourish, "that the liquid is not venom." Not venom but honey, a fact that comes to us after five pages of ingenious observation of robber bees, katydids, and others who lap up the drops after flying off—if they survive the attack. More surprisingly, Plath comes up with the evidence himself. "It has," he assures us, "a sweet taste."

Having little experience in science, I might romanticize its famous method. Still, what moves me about Otto Plath's work is its curious blankness of mind. The man seems to know nothing when he confronts the bees. In their own habitat, he waits for them *to show him something*. Then he carefully goes about finding reason. What is kept intact is wonder for the alien world. There is no knowing except gradually, firsthand.

"Spirit of my dead father, protect me," Sylvia Plath either thought, or, in writing of it, liked to think she thought, going blank herself—howbeit in a more dangerous, perhaps richer way—before the bees.

❦

We were looking for the queen now, scanning the combs for a clue. An hour had passed; I was having trouble with my helmet and veil though the wind was mild. I kept adjusting it.

The bees never stopped. (Do they ever sleep? I asked. Well, not sleep as we think it, he said. They rest maybe two minutes an hour, that is, we think they rest. They just hang motionless on the comb.) I tried to find one resting but gave it up. They seemed to have forgotten us, forgotten, that is, our smoke. Hundreds, perhaps thousands of black-winged things, layers and layers moved over the brood cells, the honey cells. They were frantic, the work surprisingly specific—nurse bees feeding the pupae and the larvae, house bees cleaning and taking out the dead, the foragers returning with pollen and honey and looking for an empty cell in the combs to discharge their treasure. At least that's what my companion told me they were doing, expertly pointing out who was who; all, to my eye, caught up in the same tiny gyrations. They made me dizzy; they looked like the onslaught of a migraine, the moment after the floating sensation has passed. They were austere and ornate and entirely self-possessed. One felt hopeless and inexact before them. I thought of Plath's poem, "The Arrival of the Bee Box":

> I put my eye to the grid.
> It is dark, dark,
> With the swarmy feeling of African hands
> Minute and shrunk for export,
> Black on black, angrily clambering.
>
> How can I let them out?
> It is the noise that appalls me most of all,

The unintelligible syllables.
It is like a Roman mob,
Small, taken one by one, but my god, together!

There it is, in that high exclamation—"but my god, to-
gether!"—the poem's heart, its moment of release. And after
the silence of the stanza break, we are returned to the
calmed down, the rational.

I lay my ear to furious Latin.
I am not a Caesar.
I have simply ordered a box of maniacs.
They can be sent back.
They can die, I need feed them nothing, I am the owner.

I wonder how hungry they are.

The rest downshifts further, full of *ifs* and misgivings and
sensible, weighted questions. "I am no source of honey," she
writes reasonably in the famous final lines,

So why should they turn on me?
Tomorrow I will be sweet God, I will set them free.

The box is only temporary.

In the first draft of this poem, however, written by hand in
Devon that last October, on pink memorandum paper she
collected years before from Smith College and on whose re-
verse side she typed *The Bell Jar*, the movement in those lines
is more complex, more open to meditative pause. She adds
two full lines.

I am no source of honey.
Tomorrow is soon enough to think of that.
Is it a brain that rages, is it a heart?
So why should they turn on me?
Tomorrow I will be sweet God, I will set them free.

The box is only temporary.

It's the third line I love, the one she crossed straight out in black ink—"Is it a brain that rages, is it a heart?" It could have been a chant, this thing she threw away.

I stooped, eye level to the hive. My companion had gone to retrieve something from the car, and I was alone with them.

❦

How does imagery take hold, what burning buried thing in us demands that return to certain rooms or gestures, certain plain nightmares and recognitions, to those and not to others, retelling them in whatever new odd focus, whatever disguise?

In a short story, written in her early twenties, Plath describes a father in a garden after supper. It amazes his small daughter, Alice, how he'd catch a bumblebee, hold it in his closed hand to her ear. She liked "the angry, stifled buzzing of the bee," Plath tells us,

> captured in the dark trap of her father's hand, but not stinging, not daring to sting. Then, with a laugh, her father would spread his fingers wide and the bee would fly out, free, up into the air and away.

In this small scene, composed and heightened as something in a locket, a whole childhood—its fear and wonder—might be compressed. The bees, a real fact of her early years given her father's work, are more than stage trappings. They are danger and romance; they claim the father even as both he and the girl who identifies with him are defined by the simple heroic light against them. "Among the Bumblebees" she called the story, though only a small bit of the piece concerns them. So images, triggered most of all, perhaps, by longing—Otto Plath died when she was eight—begin their long-term settlement in the imagination.

Meanwhile, it's impossible to figure fully what Sylvia Plath really learned about bees from her father, or whether, later, she had read his book at all. Certainly his bees were a very different sort than those that finally intrigued her. Bumblebees don't survive as a colony over winter as honeybees do, for instance (though the bumblebee queens hibernate alone). Neither do bumblebees make enough honey for people to take interest. They burrow in the earth to nest, unlike the honeybees who make their combs—things of great formal beauty in themselves—either in man-made hives or high in trees or eaves.

Yet images speak, and in two earlier bee poems—both elegies for her father, written at least three years before the bee sequence—Plath uses what she does know of her father's world. But it is grief that transforms it. In "The Beekeeper's Daughter," she borrows a detail for the last stanza that was both recorded in Otto Plath's book on bees, and, according to Ted Hughes, demonstrated to her by him. "In burrows as narrow as a finger," she writes in that poem, "solitary bees / keep house among the grasses. Kneeling down / I set my eye to the hole-mouth and meet an eye / Round, green, disconsolate as a tear." The second poem, "Electra on Azalea Path," begins more personally, and immediately rivets:

> The day you died I went into the dirt,
> Into the lightless hibernaculum
> Where bees, striped black and gold, sleep out the blizzard
> Like hieratic stones, and the ground is hard.

Mourning, of course, exacts its own stark requirements of memory, and if certain bees mimic the dead to survive, burying themselves in the rich heat of earth, they might *answer* the way metaphor *answers* in its mysterious interior equation—and therefore recovery—of things. "What do I remember / that was shaped / as this thing is shaped?" Williams asked. Things equal, they do not stop equaling. And in that swift linkage the imagination comes awake and builds, sometimes moving like the hummingbird's wing, so rapid that it appears to us motionless.

That motionless—I think Plath was that motionless, clear about survival in the bee sequence, written the October she and Ted Hughes separated, written out of knowledge of the natural world won in her own solitary way, getting a hive and keeping it in Devon where she stayed on with the children the whole nectar-gathering summer. Such a world, certainly, is a strictly feminine one. The workers are females, as, of course, is the queen. The only males—the drones—are worthless to the colony beyond their grip and prowess at high altitudes during the queen's famous bridal flight. In fact, it was the women in Devon who taught Plath the art of keeping bees. Although her neighbor, Charlie Pollard, would instruct her some and even give her one of his cast-off hives, it was her midwife, Winifred Davies, whom she relied upon for sensible advice that summer into fall, and the "blue-coated woman" from British Guiana whom she met at that first bee meeting. "Today, guess what, we've become *beekeepers!*" she wrote home that June in the manic, expansive tone she habitually used in letters to her mother. But it was true; no longer merely the beekeeper's daughter, Plath would keep bees herself. "Now bees land on my flowers," she told Elizabeth Compton Sigmund, a Devon friend, about the flowers she had painted on her hive.

Late that October, she would go to London to read and be interviewed for the BBC by Peter Orr. Although choosing not to read any of her poems about them, she spoke of the bees and the enormous value of her midwife's instruction. "I'm fascinated by this, this mastery of the practical . . . ," she told him. "I must say, I feel as a poet one lives a bit on air. . . ."

❧

It's tempting, that air. It's how one courts transcendence. So we write—as she did—mostly lyric poems. Plath's bee poems are surely that—lyrics—yet the sequence design does a curious thing: it bestows narrative rigor on the whole scary business, making its own demands for lucidity. And though each poem in the sequence might be weighted, as many critics have assumed, toward the death that would claim her only four months later, because she's worked narratively, toward *story*, we sense hope and recovery: *something this vitally begun is going to will out.*

In the handwritten manuscript, at least, the individual poems are part of a whole, each a numbered section, and though

Ted Hughes followed that order, he published them posthumously in *Ariel* as separate pieces. Either way, the shape of the sequence is dramatic, and—no tricks—it proceeds as matter-of-factly as life often does. One goes to a bee meeting for inspiration and information. Step two: one gets a box of bees. If we abstract the rest, their gist becomes as true as this, and as laughable for the reduction. In "Stings" the bees are transferred to the hive, and the queen flies off to mate; in "The Swarm" the colony has doubled and now divides; and in "Wintering" the bees hone in, clustering for heat, venturing out only on warm days to remove their dead, and thus, they live out the cold.

It's not completely ridiculous, I think, to summarize so. Her eye to the clear consecutive facts of the world allowed a leaping-off place, a frame for her personal and metaphorical invention in the poems in exactly the way that for her real narratives—her stories—it did not. "The blunt fact," wrote Ted Hughes in his introduction to her selected prose volume, "killed any power or inclination (in her) to rearrange it, to see it differently." In contrast, in these late poems, the actual bees steadied her, brought her deliciously out of that air on which, she said, poets tend to live, though perhaps that's in part because the details of the colony's life are so profoundly alien. Already the bees must have seemed surreal to her, messengers from the unspeakable inner life.

🐝

Two hours now—it was three o'clock, the sun no longer straight up but to my left. We had given up all hope of finding the queen. My companion said, hold it, handing me a slide, one of the hive's extracting frames as heavy as an early-twentieth-century X-ray. Hold it to the light, he said, like a surgeon eager to share his bright diagnosis.

It was a comb in my hand, its cells repeating endlessly, perfect and only partly waxed shut, so much of it a lovely gold. Honey, of course, glossy and dazzling, even without the sun behind it.

This was the *after*; the *before* was Plath's:

He and I

Have a thousand clean cells between us,
Eight combs of yellow cups,
And the hive itself a teacup. . . .

It's spring in these lines, all possibility, even though—
unseen—the queen is "old / Her wings torn shawls, her long
body / Robbed of its plush—" even though the brood cells
from which new workers and drones and future queens will
come to "terrify" and look like "wormy mahogany." What
draws me is the doubt and wonder, an unlikely combination.
And in her fine-nerved phrasing questions mix with personal
flashes, forcing the facts of the colony's life upward into a
human orbit. "I stand in a column," Plath tells us,

Of winged, unmiraculous women,
Honey-drudges.
I am no drudge
Though for years I have eaten dust
And dried plates with my dense hair.

And seen my strangeness evaporate,
Blue dew from dangerous skin.
Will they hate me,
These women who only scurry,
Whose news is the open cherry, the open clover?

It is almost over.
I am in control.
Here is my honey-machine,
It will work without thinking. . . .

The lost queen finally does emerge, and in that we have
the heart of the bee sequence, its climactic revelation. After
the entrance and exit of the so-called "third person," after the
high spinning pitch of questions ("Is she dead, / Is she sleep-
ing? / Where has she been, / With her lion-red body, her
wings of glass?"), we're charged for the simple triumph of
that final stanza, its *now* dropping down with the weight of
stunned discovery.

Now she is flying
More terrible than she ever was, red
Scar in the sky, red comet
Over the engine that killed her—
The mausoleum, the wax house.

"The great appeal of *Ariel* and its constellated lyrics," Seamus Heaney has written, "is the feeling of irresistible givenness. There inheres in this poetry a sense of surprised arrival, of astonished being." But that arrival, in the poem "Stings" at least, was a tedious, hard-earned matter of starts and stops, at first more a creature of autobiography than poetic urgency.

Enter again the "third person." During Mr. Pollard's installation of their new swarm, "Ted had only put a handkerchief over his head where the hat should go in the bee mask," Plath wrote to her mother that June, "and the bees crawled into his hair, and he flew off with a half-a-dozen stings. I didn't get stung at all, and when I went back to the hive later, I was delighted to see bees entering with pollen sacs full and leaving with them empty—at least I *think* that's what they were doing."

In Plath's final rendering of "Stings," written four months later in October, the incident, however detailed, is reduced to episode, a kind of dismissal in her summary. Her fascination remains with the bees and the subsequent images of self she borrows from their passionate activity. Translated from prose to poem, the third person "has nothing to do with the bee seller or with me—" Plath writes. "Now he is gone."

In eight great bounds, a great scapegoat.
Here is his slipper, here is another
And here the square of white linen
He wore instead of a hat.
He was sweet,

The sweat of his efforts a rain
Tugging the world to fruit.
The bees found him out,
Molding onto his lips like lies,
Complicating his features.

> They thought death was worth it, but I
> Have a self to recover, a queen. . . .

In the first version of this poem begun two months earlier in August, the intent is narrower; the piece completely circles this "third person"—he is the magnetic figure, another "maestro of the bees," as Plath remembered her father in an earlier poem, though this time the heroic shine is drastically altered. It begins:

> What honey in you summons these animalcules.
> What fear? It has set them zinging.
> Zinging & zinging on envious strings, & you are the center.
> They are assailing your brain like numbers,
> They are in your hair.

> Under the white handkerchief you wore instead of a hat.
> They are making a cat's cradle, they are suicidal.
> Their death-pegs stud your gloves, it is no use running.
> The black veil molds to your lips:
> They think they must kiss you, they think death is worth
> it. . . .

Last winter, when I came upon this handwritten draft in the Smith College manuscript collection, that initial line stopped me; I felt, for the first time, the deep quiet in the room. "What honey in you summons these animalcules? / What fear?" I read again. But "summons" is scribbled above her original choice, "attracts," which is energetically crossed out. *Attracts*, the word is wide and safe, nearing straight description. But *summons*—it's as focused as desire, helpless as dream. I stared at the exacting transformation, this change of "attracts" right before me into the terrible, almost wordless *summons*. I stood there over the manuscript; strangers walked by me, all cast shadows on the page. I recalled a conversation with a friend, our shared annoyance with Plath's impulse to jerk everything toward melodrama, this habit of enlarging by compressing, of intensifying into nightmare for release.

I looked back to the line; the change was definitive, utterly characteristic of both the worst of Plath, and the best. *Summons*—amazing to me how one word upped the ante, made everything instantly strange and interior, impossible to stop. I felt witness to that click, right there, a visible shift, this quickening from major to minor key so close to that moment of "astonished being" that Heaney speaks of. In the last year of her life, Plath wrote a brief childhood memoir, and in that account recalled being read a poem of Matthew Arnold's— "Forsaken Merman"—when she was very small:

I saw gooseflesh on my skin. I did not know what made it. I was not cold. Had a ghost passed over me? No, it was the poetry. A spark flew off Arnold and shook me, like a chill. I wanted to cry; I felt very odd. I had fallen into a new way of being happy.

❦

Happiness then, some brief definitions: "Like this," my companion was saying, the hives behind us now as we walked toward the car. "I held my arms up like this"—and still in gloves and bee mask, he stood radiant, embracing the fall air. I had asked about swarming; his face came alive through the veil. "In May, or early June," he told me. "And one time, I was right here when they started, thousands pouring out, all at once." I imagined them passing over him, a dark cloud of bees, all frantic purpose upward until he was a small, motionless figure way below, his arms still open, letting them go. "The bees have got so far, seventy feet high!" wrote Plath in her poem "The Swarm," euphoric and at eye level with her own rising bees: "Russia, Poland and Germany! / The mild hills, the same old magenta / Fields shrunk to a penny / spun into a river, the river crossed. . . ." So years and places drop away in the associative flash of such flight, here—Europe's ancient miseries, its deliberate smiling tyrants. What ghost passes over us when we write? "A flying hedgehog," she called the raging colony, "all prickles. . . ."

❦

Plath had a plan for *Ariel*, a map for its long chill and peculiar joy. As Grace Schulman has written, so many of its poems were works "of praise," howbeit "a fearful praise." According to Ted Hughes, Plath herself marked its boundaries with two words: *love* to begin ("Love set you going like a fat gold watch" from "Morning Song" about her newborn daughter) and *spring*, from the final line of "Wintering," to end the book. So the bee sequence would go last, a design Hughes put aside when publishing the collection to finish instead with the inscrutable stark double take of poems written later, "Edge" and "Words." In retrospect, given the fact of her suicide, Hughes' order illustrates, gives reason perhaps, but as both Marjorie Perloff and Linda Wagner have argued, it dishonors intent, and with that, the real triumph of the book.

Plath's own shape for the collection was a hopeful one, but admittedly, the active turn toward spring—at least in the last poem of her sequence—seems to have come as a surprise to her. That poem, "Wintering," is, of course, steadied throughout by domestic detail and necessity. The hive has to be set for winter, the bees fed watered sugar, the honey extracted and put in cellar jars ("next to the last tenant's rancid jam," she tells us, "and the bottles of empty glitters—Sir So-and-So's gin"). The bees themselves in the poem behave as operatically as they do in life, clustering for warmth, removing their dead from the combs, evicting, without a pause, the live males, the drones—"the blunt, clumsy stumblers, the boors," Plath calls them—who now add nothing to the colony's welfare. This purposeful female world hones in to survive, a fact no doubt not lost on the poet, estranged at this point from the marriage that sustained her for six years. "Winter is for women—" she writes in haunting summary. "The woman, still at her knitting, / at the cradle of Spanish walnut, / her body a bulb in the cold and too dumb to think."

But that expansive leap toward spring in the final stanza stuns, breaks through this static sorrow. And if we can believe the several manuscript drafts that still exist, moving eerily as time-lapse camera work, it was authentic liberation from her dirgelike habit.

> Will the hive survive, will the gladiolas
> Succeed in banking their fires

To enter another year?
What will they taste of, the Christmas roses?—

In all versions, including the last, this much stands whole.
It is with the stanza's last two lines that she struggled. Draft
one:

What will they taste of, the Christmas roses?
Snow water? Corpses?

To this she added, "A Sweet spring?" but crossed it out.
"Spring?"—left intact. "Impossible spring?" crossed out. "What
sort of spring?"—crossed out. "O God, let them taste of
spring" crossed out. By the third draft, things had moved into
typescript, and the final line into frozen, fully tragic images:
Snow water? Corpses? A glass wing?

But even here, though "snow water" and "corpses" re-
main, the glass wing has several lines through it, and hand-
written then, at wild angles, are all her spinning options, her
stop-start movement toward the right transcendent gesture
that will end the poem: "A gold bee, flying?"—crossed out.
"Resurrected"—crossed out. "Bee-song?"—crossed out. "Or
a bee flying"—crossed out. Everything, in short, crossed out
until, in a jubilant cursive—"The bees are flying. They taste
the spring."

One great leap remains; the whole stanza is dismissed with
an elegant wavy line, and typed beneath is the full published
version—with one crucial correction. Plath's oppressive stand-
still litany—"Snow water? Corpses?"—is violently crossed out,
that final line completely given over to the bees and their
dizzy upward release:

Will the hive survive, will the gladiolas
Succeed in banking their fires
To enter another year?
What will they taste of, the Christmas roses?
The bees are flying. They taste the spring.

❧

All the way home in the car, I could still hear them in my head, their low-grade buzzing, indifferent to whatever joy or grief we make of their sound, in poems or out of them. And for the rest of the day, I couldn't shake the memory of something. Slowly it came back to me, the way dreams do, in flashes.

I remembered waiting in a car, alone, having gone with a friend to pick up her son from his violin lesson. To my right, and down into a meadow, I saw three stacks of white boxes, three hives. The boy was still playing; I could hear the sweet barbed threat of it, that edgy quarreling sound he made, and sometimes a note held so high it disappeared. I kept my ear there, in a trance, a kind of manageable beauty. Even so, something in the meadow drew me; my eye kept returning to it, some busy darkness I could only imagine. For several minutes the boy played. One side of things, and then the other. Unlike Plath, I couldn't begin to balance it.

The Sound of It

This first, which might doom everything: poetry is the closest literary form we have to silence. I think about prose too sometimes. What I think is—prose is made almost completely of words. And poetry is not. I keep coming back to this notion in more visceral ways, especially these warmer mornings, the windows open, all the early neighborhood silence rushing in. But of course that silence, like poetry's, isn't silence at all. I hear all manner of birds—the robin's clear push-me, pull-me song, the whirl of the wren and the house finch, the plaintive two or three notes of the chickadee, the two note hiccup rush of the titmouse. Count more: the thump of the paper on the porch, the guy across the street slamming his car door once, twice. I hear my husband and son sleeping in rooms beyond this one. Such an ordinary world. Not the sound of poetry. Not yet anyway. Still the wayward, sometimes urgent sound of such a world is specifically—to me—a poetic sound, neither the mind's nor the heart's but some weird hybrid, a rhythm out to discover what is knowable and more aptly perhaps, what is not.

There are two sounds here then, and both depend a lot on knowledge and a lot on ignorance. But I want to begin at a more ancient sound than poetry, as long ago as the Ice Age when the evolution for some on this planet slowed to the point of appearing, to us anyway, virtually stopped. To get there, I need only to think past any window to the birds again, their astonishing varied sound, their small, earnest sometime snarling ways which nevertheless endure.

All spring they were my favorite secret as I slipped out of my office to audit an ornithology class, bicycling half way across the Purdue campus to the old Forestry building where their compatriots filled the hallway's tall glass cases, marbled-eyed, perfectly stuffed, sweetly vacant—those doves and vireos, hawks and towhees, all manner of bright but fading waterfowl, a vulture, a meadowlark, three distinctly disgruntled looking wrens. I remember one morning in particular, our teacher, Paul Dubowey, standing before us holding the tape recorder and playing over and over, full speed and unto its eeriest, slowed down by a quarter, then a half, the ancient song of the wood thrush, deep woods dweller, bird hidden in leaf-shade, the dark of the forest floor. The clear emphatic notes coming first, he told us, were territorial. They announced to friend or foe his presence. And the lovely haunting trill that followed? For the mate, he said. And often, listening, we lose it because really it is finished off so quietly, nearly whispered, the mate, after all, being near. And again he played the song for us, transforming that simple room with its clunky overhead and its crooked venetian blinds, changing winter itself, the snow still hanging on outside, to deep summer, all its flickering and old complexities pulling us under.

I had this bad habit: I kept thinking he was talking about poetry. After a while, I raised my hand. Does every song of every species carry within it these two dimensions, public and private? We don't know, he said. Does every poem? I thought. And as with the wood thrush, are there ways, fast or slow, to hear it? What's curious about the trill is that the bird actually sings contrasting notes simultaneously; he harmonizes with himself, thus the eerie richness of the song. The human equivalent would be overtone singing, the chant—and spiritual exercise—of some Tibetan monks. Even so, as much as we are able to make out, an enormous amount goes on in the trill that we cannot hear, past our tonal range, moving so rapidly. Thus the slowed down version our teacher played to enable that hearing. Thus, in poetry, the slowed down version scansion delivers, that fascinating, infuriating habit of prosody that allows us to blame happiness on the quick breathless anapest, or sorrow on the lamenting trochee—a measured sound for every mood or point of view, for every raised eyebrow or wry look.

What struck me first was the presence of the private dimension, how for the wood thrush anyway, intimacy followed the public declaration and its deliberate self-consciousness; that once released from that spotlight, the song cascades down to a whisper in the most intricate way. Two kinds of beauty then: monochromatic, sure, emphatic—in short, public. And the quickened, more delicate private sound. In conversation, or even more formal discourse, much of our pleasure comes in the constant play between these worlds—the aside, urgent or languid, against the matter-of-fact delivery of pure information, or a joke wedged in to give heart where it is needed.

That poetry always moves between these two states of being isn't surprising though whatever the final shape, its inward impulse is clear, and probably dominant. A few years ago Donald Hall wrote of it this way: "A poem is human inside talking to human inside. It may also be reasonable person talking to reasonable person, but if it is not inside talking to inside, it is not a poem. This inside speaks through the second language of poetry, the unintended language . . . (which) allows poetry to be universal."

This inwardness in poetry, particularly lyric poetry, may seem an obvious thing but what sharpens the idea is this notion of origin—*unintended* language, the *second* language in a poem, the part, in short, that is often neither planned nor willed. This is especially striking in formal verse where the public "reasonable person" lines are drawn so rigidly and the poet's job is to keep that perfect fit, nearly. On that *nearly*, one stakes a lot—the energy in the poem, for one. Its spirit, its life, its will to live, separate from the form's insistence to keep going. *Nearly* means to fail a little, to mess it up a little, to do a necessary small violence against the comfort of the set pattern. I like Elizabeth Bishop's skewed notion of the villanelle, for instance. Her eccentricities are particularly welcome in this form whose repetition and pace historically have suggested more of a country dance—skittish, charming, forgettable—than the rhythm of grief, though certainly this century's poets have tried memorably and well to change that, Dylan Thomas and Theodore Roethke among them. But the *reasonable* language of Bishop's poem "One Art," its public element, à la the wood thrush, does in fact keep faith with that fourteenth-century tradition of the light touch, the airy gesture.

Though not quite. Always, in Bishop, is this "not quite"—one of the reasons her work is admired, surely a reason why it is loved, keeping the scale human in this genre—poetry—where it is particularly threatened by all manner of ballooning ambitions. The actual sound suggests that human scale, a balance where slowly the private more quirky, and gradually darker rhythms undermine and finally overtake the villanelle's inherited and rather winsome, orderly patterns. At first, she goes along, offhand, appearing profoundly unserious about her losses, her poem a list of those losses, mostly, at first anyway, trivial rather than truer sorrows. "The art of losing isn't hard to master," she begins—

> So many things seem filled with the intent
> to be lost that their loss is no disaster.

And so go quickly, almost comically, the first three stanzas, the *inside* voice just one of the casual layers that begins to make the sound ironic the way one low tone is only a part, say, of a three note chord. But in that resonance we hear the wood thrush's private overtone song once more, a complication that only seems like harmony.

> Lose something everyday. Accept the fluster
> of lost door keys. The hour badly spent.
> The art of losing isn't hard to master.
>
> Then practice losing farther, losing faster.
> Places, and names, and where it was you meant
> to travel. None of these will bring disaster.

The seriousness picks up to counterpoint this witty surface; not yet a matter of imagery, it's in the sound of the words themselves. Against the various comforts of the villanelle—our expectation now of rhyme and similar sounding, if not identical, phrases—something is shifting. One hears it in the way the dark of words like "losing" and "disaster" resist the playful intent of that seemingly lucky, happy-ever-after rhyme.

But other words have an ominous feel, and begin to change our expectations of a simple good time. "Accept the fluster /" Bishop tells us in the second stanza, "of lost door keys," an amusing line not only because loss, capital L, hardly equals this sort of annoyance—lost keys hardly an occasion for the rending of garments—but because the play is in the actual sound of that word "fluster," the consonant's slapstick sound, fussy and physical, the *s* overwhelming. In spite of that, the word increases in power because of its presence at the line's end, probably the key position for reverie or revelation in any stanza since the built-in sudden pause, especially against the get-on-with-it rush of enjambment, is a surprising stillness, a place where thought—read *second thought*—pools, however briefly. Still, given the light touch of "fluster" its place of power seems facetious, part of the comedy and we appear to be pretty much where the first stanza left us, in the realm of wit rather than heart. Back and forth—perhaps we're deeper than we know into the villanelle's serious play. Surely that curious enjambment foreshadows something. Its pause allows one to think again and reconsider, sounding down a few octaves where deeper, more urgent things might lie.

Such pause is only half the treasure. The way structure itself releases powerful emotional charges has equally to do with that mysterious matter of stress as the sentences break and thread their wayward way down through the lines. Denise Levertov, in her essay on the line, points to the way such breaks insist on a "fractional pause"—managing real change in "the pitch pattern," patterns that, she goes on to say, "create significant, expressive melody, not just a pretty tune in the close tone-range of speech." *Observe the score*, she demands, her phrase itself a fierce two-stress dictum.

In Bishop's score, the threatening undertow fully begins in the third stanza. One needs to practice losing in larger ways— "places," Bishop tells us, "and names, and where it was you meant / to travel." Here we idle momentarily on that single syllable—"where it was you meant / to travel," "meant" so poignant to the human ear partly because it is almost entirely made up of heartfelt vowels and liquid consonants, sounds which rise from a place we can only imagine deep inside the body. The single stress of the word, particularly given the meditative pull and pause of enjambment, gives it a rough solitary feel, the primal feel one finds in Old English's monosyllabic rhythm before the French arrived to complicate and decorate with their many syllables. And the *t* in "meant," almost a half-syllable itself if said slowly enough, is a great part of the long wake behind this simple word, the *tss* sound carrying a whisper forward, if not true tone. Such a word mimes with its sound actual longing which is the sweet and wounded meaning of the word: all those things we *meant* to do but did not, or could not, or would not. They exist in dream. Then even the dream vanishes.

So the dark emotional force of Bishop's poem begins fully to exact its counterweight. One hears clearly in such changes her famous "movement of mind," as if she might agree with Charles Olson, from his equally famous "Projective Verse" essay, that "the ear, which is so close to the mind, that it is the mind's, . . . has the mind's speed." Here it rises, and goes abrupt, then soothing, rises again, a music increasingly layered and disturbing.

> I lost my mother's watch. And look! my last, or
> next to last, of three loved houses went.
> The art of losing isn't hard to master.
>
> I lost two cities, lovely ones. And vaster,
> some realms I owned, two rivers, a continent.
> I miss them, but it wasn't a disaster.
>
> —Even losing you (the joking voice, a gesture
> I love) I shan't have lied. It's evident
> the art of losing's not too hard to master
> though it may look like (*Write it!*) like disaster.

Though the wit, the public "reasonable person" sound continues in the rhyme, in the playful exclamations and hyperbole, and in the effort, still, to be offhand, even amused by detail large and small, a private sorrow grows larger, more visible. We see it in the imagery but by the final stanza, which begins with the urgent dash that Dickinson loved, we are entirely in the presence of human grief, its unmistakable sound, every line enjambed now to honor its silence, its awkward, heart-stopping hesitations.

❧

Evening now, and upstairs, my son is practicing his cello, an instrument he inexplicably loves, though not more than running, not more than geography. It's Bach he loves these days, those intricate patterns that move like lace being made quickly, the hand blurring as one watches, or later, the way light is held and released in the loose weave hung in a window, casting a dizzy shadow on the table, on the good wood floor. But my son has trouble with each piece at first, struggling to read it right, not the notes so much—he knows those—but the way they move along in time, some lingering, some as brief as a wing beat, against the steady undertone coming in four beats, four beats. I hear him stop and complain and call his father from the other room. I hear them there, patiently counting out the lines together, then whistling those lines until what first seemed only so many evenly spaced notes is suddenly shaped—through rich unpredictable pattern—to song. As much silence in any long held note, in that pause, as sound.

A few basic claims, then, about time. Whatever music does, or poems do, they at the very least measure time—slow it or speed it up, making the imagined shape of things the real shape. Bach is both pendulum-slow and so fast, he blurs. One riff could prove that. And so, in a line of poetry, either formal or free verse, many unstressed syllables *seem* faster than a few stressed ones though—here's the weird catch—the actual time elapsed is the same. Consider Hopkins breathless—"As king-fishers catch fire, dragonflies draw flame"—and Hopkins slow—"I wake and feel the fall of dark, not day." Both lines from poems whose base rhythm is pentameter, five real stresses in each line, but the first is the poet in his ecstatic mode, the second in his late despair, time itself actually experienced differently. Five beats, however, is still five beats, meaning stresses—meaning, Harvey Gross has ingeniously pointed out, five "isochronous intervals"—which is to say, slight pauses to the English ear, steadying the line no matter how much energy is flung out through the unstressed beats, happily dissipated in the ecstatic line, or how compressed and held close the despairing monosyllabic rhythm might seem.

If this is illusion, then the lie serves an emotional truth and, in Hopkins' case at least, illustrates the poet's passion, great flights or great depths of realization, nothing in between. If it seems mere trick, then poetry isn't the only culprit. Gross, for one, compares painters and poets; the illusion of space that perspective offers, a couple of inches on canvas, say, easily equaling a half mile of gravel road. So the rhythm in a line suggests time passing. But there are other small mysteries. One hears the pressure on the phrasing itself as it works against the forward, measured movement of the lines. A two syllable word, for instance, that moves ahead to the next foot, crosses what's called the "foot boundary" making the line seem to speed up while a word that stays within such a boundary will considerably slow things down—another slight of hand.

Fast or slow, perhaps these have long been in the catalog of ways silence plays itself off against sound, the stay-no-go-no-stay impulse in poetry. But silence shows itself in other ways in our language besides tempo. Audiologists tell us how the sound of *nothing* makes up a large part of what we say, the way pure air spins out in certain consonants, those *s*s and *p*s that carry only a little way, scattering thin and long as light. But it's more than that. Harvey Gross has written that any repetition is to some degree a "vocalized pause," not only to underscore but to savor certain moments of realization, make them stay. Driving around Indianapolis near dark once, in a car full of writers, I remember our joy when we realized we all knew Robert Hayden's poem "Those Winter Sundays" and launched in, reciting it carefully, reverently as chant. "Sundays too my father got up early," we began, coming in midstory with the exactitude of that small word "too," as if already intimate with the scene that gradually and with great reserved beauty unfolds in praise of this father "in the blue-black cold" whose "hands ached / from labor in the week-day weather." And "No one ever thanked him," certainly not the teenage son the speaker once was, who only spoke "indifferently to him." What I mainly recall was slowing at this point—the light had turned red—and Susan Neville uncharacteristically still for a moment behind the steering wheel, throwing her head back, as we all half sang, half whispered the glorious end of that poem—"What did I know, what did I know / of love's austere and lonely offices?" And in that ending echoing phrase—certainly *a vocalized pause*—a restless gravity somehow mimes and thus deepens regret into sorrow, giving it sound.

Really what we are up against here, again, is time itself, how human thought unfolds in a poem, how it is held privately then released moment by real moment, how sound is a key measure of that release, not only orchestrating the order of our realizations but to a large extent their nature. The pacing, after all, is what we pick up first and probably last. I recall Grace Schulman telling me once about her experience with Marianne Moore, a close friend of her family it turns out, as well as the subject of a valuable study she did of her work. After Moore's series of small strokes late in life, Schulman was one of the few who could easily understand the poet's garbled speech. After so many conversations and taped interviews done in preparation for her book, playing those reel-to-reel tapes backward and forward, slowing them down to pick up every nuance, she would know instantly that the incomprehensible something Moore was uttering was "how is your mother?" or "Do I look well?" It was the pace and maybe the cadence; it was the rush of the whole of it, after years and years of hard and affectionate listening.

The *whole of it*, then. That's what haunts, and finally matters. Because if poetic structure is largely patterns of sound, it can't only be a matter of line, this timing of syllable and phrase, when to repeat or not to repeat, when to know how a mid- or end-line pause weights just enough. There's the sound of the whole argument or declaration, not program music merely to illustrate plot but the actual sound of human expectation and resolution in the way poems open and continue and end, all mirroring the stunningly different ways we experience what the world offers us, day by day, not rotely. Still it has been argued for years that poems follow however faintly or perversely the basic form in music, the ABA form, theme-variation-theme, the old wisdom of the fugue, the concerto, the sonata, which Coleridge said was devoted to the reconciliation of opposites, of dissonance. Helen Vendler, in a review-essay she did for the *New Republic* a few years back, mentioned that there was a specific, and surely annoying, sentimental sound in poems, different, I assume, from the merely plaintive or reflective though she didn't say. It might have something to do with following too literally, too patly—in terms of sound at least—this sonata formula, this will to resolve all differences. Since the review concerned a biography of Sylvia Plath—who was many things though "sentimental" almost never comes to mind—Coleridge's remark seems especially right, though somehow altered in the translation from music to poetry, the poem's dissonance not to be untangled, at least not completely.

But the old sonata form sometimes makes sense, especially as a poem tends to complication, as it pushes forward, even in a piece heavily laced with memory that itself exacts a counterpressure on that movement. Before long we are headed for the heart of things, the troubling middle. This is the B section of the ABA rondo form; its presence messes things up, contrasts, rethinks the thought. Weldon Kees, a poet among many other things—musician, painter, journalist, librarian, photographer—wrote what to me is a perfect poem in this regard. His "1926" is compact, only fifteen lines, three five-line stanzas, but enormous things go on there, equivalent maybe, to managing Brueghel's "Fall of Icarus" on the head of a pin, with its demands of space and time and memorable silence.

The poem is, in fact, a miniature time machine, terribly elastic in its jumps and turns, though the first stanza seems ordinary enough, devoted to immediate place and season: the present tense suggests this. "The porchlight coming on again," Kees begins in a steady stately rhythm.

> Early November, the dead leaves
> Raked in piles, the wicker swing
> Creaking. Across the lots
> A phonograph is playing *Ja-Da*.

After that first line, nothing is end stopped anymore, the continual enjambment forcing its familiar tension of pause against the rush of the sentence as it winds into the next line. The single stress of virtually all the end line words—leaves, swings, lots—works somewhat as the "where it was you meant / to travel" does in Bishop's "One Art," setting up a particular kind of sorrow and reserve though the sheer number of these single stress words makes the rhythm far heavier, almost dirge. And each line turns to meet no rest, only first stresses again—"dead leaves / raked" and "wicker swing / creaking," the sound narrowed and heightened by the emphasis granted any first place position. In this way, we've entered the tears of things. One *hears* that even without the press of the old neighborhood, how it was there in the last desolate days of fall, at the ghostly swing, listening to the distant disembodied song coming from the phonograph. The curious repeated combination of pause and emphatic stress works reverie and expectation equally. Something is about to happen. But everything is remote, secret, hardly human. And in the long pause between stanzas, we drift on that strangeness, the slow vowel stress of the *Ja-Da* still faint, an echo.

The brilliant entry into voice, not mere setting, comes with the simple three-stressed fragment that begins stanza two, the eye expertly drawn up by the image, "An orange moon." What might have gone on as plain story is abruptly altered. We know that by what we do not hear, which is to say, no full sentence now, nothing so reasonable. We've gone inward to the unexpected, the broken off. For the first time, a speaker enters, drawn, it seems, by trance.

> I see the lives
> Of neighbors, mapped and marred
> Like all the wars ahead, and R.
> Insane, B. with his throat cut,
> Fifteen years from now in Omaha.

Suddenly this present tense is clearly the eternal present that includes the past, and astonishingly, the future too, the speaker seeing himself as the child he was—one begins to take the title "1926" quite literally—and at the same moment, someone who knows what will happen, death already revealed in its terrible and specific disguises, the way only memory knows. The way, one might add, only poetry knows with its unyielding sense of the infinite. On this point, Russell Edson once wrote a remarkable essay—"The Prose Poem in America"—exploring the ways poetry differs from prose, betting that difference on how we experience time, which, he said, "flows *through* prose, and *around* poetry." Prose is used up in this way, "bringing things into existence, only to have them disappear down into the end of the plot," thus an inevitably "tragic" form, whereas poetry, as gloomy as even this piece by Kees might be, remains "inherently joyous" working out of "a sense of the permanent, of time held."

Although not a prose poet like Edson, Kees uses prose elements—scene, character—to suggest, howbeit skewed, time passing, the tragedy of our knowledge concerning that. But sequence is not respected; the shard-like flashing middle stanza throws our normal sense of things into a small, truthful madness. One can barely hold it in the mind. That particular grasp of time is perhaps one of the reasons "1926" seems cast in dream, profoundly disorienting and all-at-once, the way the blind see when sight is restored midlife and they must deal with space as well as time, concentrating slowly and hard on the separate parts of things to grasp anything at all.

One could say that's simply the imagery at work, coming at us in high contrast since this isn't a narrative; there is no time for description or connectives. But the sound is highly monosyllabic—dirge unto drumbeats, death counted and weighted. Its slow motion is a public sound, yet the long sentence rush of it seems utterly private, visionary, breathless in the summary way it marks event. Oddly, the dominant sound is the soothing iambic—the rest *before* the strike and then the rest again—though there are enough first-syllable-stress trochaic and spondaic moments to unsettle things and deepen urgency: "B. with his throat cut / Fifteen years from now in Omaha."

As in dream, one eventually wakes. And we are back to basic, more obvious measures, almost all of them neatly end-stopped, complete, plain sentences of fact, the iambic now certainly underpinning everything.

> I did not know them then.
> My airedale scratches at the door.
> And I am back from seeing Milton Sills
> And Doris Kenyon. Twelve years old.
> The porchlight coming on again.

In the repetition of the poem's first line for the last, we have a willfully quiet drama, a "vocalized pause," the nature of that light transformed forever. In the scene repeated and returning us to the first stanza—the detail of the house, the dog, the porch again—it is theme-variation-theme, in part the sonata form but the dissonance and its sadness is not resolved à la Coleridge's expectation. Here the speaker darkly and without nostalgia witnesses for real the oblivious child he was, coming home from the movies on an ordinary moonlit night. That the chilling weight of our century lay before him, that he is ignorant and innocent, changes any light we try to see by. So in this poem whose habit and scale seem at first domestic and private, the pressure of history enters. And irony. And larger things, like a wonder so pure it exists without joy.

The direct and simple phrasing is misleading. The physicist Stephen Hawking is fond of asking and basing his amazing work on what seem to be foolish questions. One is: why don't we remember the future as we do the past? The way tense shifts in the troubling middle of this piece without *seeming* to, the way we stand there with the speaker in the present and past and future all at once, the astonishment of such a moment owes much to the way the enjambed lines break the tableau of stanza one, the eerie *struck* sound of the initials instead of names, the tough and tight-lipped monosyllabic reserve that carries all this forward. There's pathos in this, and, as in Bishop's poem, human scale. This piece could have resolved itself in spectacularly self-aggrandizing and sentimental ways, ways, in short, that make what is private inappropriately and glad-handedly public. The fact that it does not, that it maintains what it stubbornly does not know is a great part of that. In her review-essay, Helen Vendler turned to what she considered an ethical issue, the "heroic struggle" in writing what she calls "accurate art," a matter "of refusing the false, the strained, the untransformed, the sentimental, the bombastic, the self-serving, the deceitful, the institutionally approved." And refusing these things "not only thematically and stylistically, but structurally and rhythmically." So "1926" is Weldon Kees' refusal—the troubling images but also the modest, damning elegance of its sound.

❦

An eternal, uneasy alliance perhaps, this thing between image and sound, what is visible and what's not. In the dark of the mind, past image, one hears things—different, I think, than simply *listening for*. One might be startled awake at night, say, by hearing things, and spend a long time after waiting for whatever sound it was to come again. In that second state, one collects and recollects and is soothed by the expected: the clock ticking downstairs and chiming the hour, a car outside braking gradually, the windows and their rattle even in small winds because the house is old, warped by time and weather. But all art—perhaps all anything—is made up of two simple elements, Ezra Pound liked to hold forth, the fixed and the variable. Very quickly then, the fixed becomes these background sounds on such a night. And the threatening variant that might come again, any minute—a sparrow lost in the dryer vent? a picture wire snapping? an honest-to-god thief?—becomes the center of one's adrenalin, one's attention, one's waking dream. Certainly one could argue this is life not art. But other things are not so clearly set apart. Concerning sounds that birds make, for instance, the old theory is easy and probably close to Pound's idea. Although there are calls and buzzes, all sorts of repetitive noise, it's the *variant*, which is to say, the unexpected, which carries immediate life. That makes it song.

Or poetry. Once a few years ago, I heard Michael Ryan offer to play a section from "The Waste Land" after giving a talk at Warren Wilson College on Eliot. Oh, "The Waste Land," I thought, thinking I hadn't read it in years, remembering with some dread those footnotes, and Eliot's "big voice," a decidedly public sound that pretty much set the pace and sound of poetry readings for decades, that ponderous intonation, the monotonous rising pitch of each line from which we've never quite recovered. Still, I decided to stay, and sitting there, back to the wall, I instantly recognized the unmistakable St. Louis native turned proper English banker booming out his extraordinary witness to a failed culture, a failed century—at least its first decade or two. Happily, the distance of twenty some years from the routine adoration offered the man was an outright gift, helping me go blank enough finally to *hear* the poem, not merely to be polite and appreciate.

What I heard, I think now, was the variant. And it shocked me. Amid Eliot's weighty chairman-of-the-board, near Olympian pitch and tempo came the private, vulnerable, and disembodied voices—the child's cry coming up quickly—"And I was frightened. He said, Marie, / Marie, hold on tight. And down we went"—or later, the Hyacinth girl, or the fortune teller running blandly through her routine—"I do not find / The Hanged Man. Fear death by water. / I see crowds of people walking round in a ring. / Thank you. If you see dear Mrs. Equitone. . . ." Since then, I've heard other recordings that seem to me more of a piece, but in that tape, I recall my surprise, particularly, at the amazing turns: the child's voice— Eliot trying to manage a falsetto and doing it badly—the bored teller of fortunes, then back to the old great poet voice that lifts or chills, or annoys. These odd quick starts and stops seemed to make no sense. A fragmentary sound—that is no surprise; it's deep in the ear already of anyone born in this century, its desire, its way of *scoring* despair, but this? I was actually hearing it *make no sense*. Suddenly Eliot seemed just someone come around to read his new poem for the first time and everyone thinking, not happily—*What the . . .?* And just as suddenly I was struck by something absolutely required in any great work: the utter nerve of its sequence. Not lofty ambition or learned footnotes, not its grown-up, elegant nod to biblical cadence and history and literary tradition but sheer looniness. Which is less a matter of image than sound—the sound, for Eliot, of actual speech, its uncertainty and indiffer-

ence, against his trademark heavily stressed and tracelike ru-
minations that seem so much the high public sound of
thought. I flashed again on the shock that must have regis-
tered when it was first heard, before Eliot's canonization hit
and no one questioned anymore. A little perhaps like the
shock of the audience, confused and even angry on hearing
Beethoven's Third Symphony for the first time—not a thing
like Haydn!—or later their reaction to Tchaikovsky when
they were used to Beethoven.

In hearing Eliot this way, I was hearing—to use Hopkins'
fine distinction on this, made in a letter to his friend A. W. M.
Baille—"the language of inspiration," a poet actually using
"the gift of genius" which "raises him above himself." The
normal, everyday ground level where a great poet usually
lived, Hopkins called "Parnassian," the mark of which—he
wonderfully says—is "that one could conceive oneself writing
it if one were that poet," things "spoke on and from the level
of (that) poet's mind." No more, or less, than that. Too much
Parnassian, however, and a poet's work palls on us. "We seem
to have found out his secret," Hopkins writes. It becomes, in
short, "too so-and-so-all-overish to be quite inspiration." I
knew, seemingly by heart, what Eliot sounds like. Which is to
say, I knew his *Parnassian*: what was predictable. What I hadn't
heard was the place where he probably surprised himself,
suddenly, to shape time differently.

Robert Hass has a brief thought—more wonder than
thought—in one of his essays as he considers large changes in
rhythmic form, not poem by poem or even poet by poet, but
whole washes of poetic sound as decades turn to centuries. Of
the great sea change that most affects us—the move in the
nineteenth and early twentieth centuries against strict metri-
cal verse—he finds "an astonishing psychological fact, as if a
huge underpinning in the order of things had given way, and
where men had heard the power of incantatory repetition
before, they now heard the monotony. Or worse." The nature
of this shift, as Hass himself admits, is probably too large and
complex to grasp. Consider Whitman one day giving up the
waltz to stride resolutely and unashamed to the ends of his
long lines. Not variant merely in releasing a mad dactyl or two

to mess up the reliable iambic line, or even variant to register emotion in the nervous system where these things echo and reverberate, but variant as profound change in cultural perspective coming via sound—*Hold on tight, Marie!* Even the sonorous, tradition-wielding Eliot on board.

Variant—more of the private, the largely unintended element in that, than public. More "inside person" than reasonable sound in our poems. At the same time, more and more an effort to be sincere, sincerity itself probably the dominant impulse of the last forty years or so in American poetry. And who can say, as we so confidently do about the effect of Whitman (and Dickinson, his alter ego) on the nineteenth century, exactly who the emblem poets of our age might be? I think about Berryman sometimes, shard master of this century's peculiar longing, both sincere and more importantly—the variant—his resisting, *almost* successfully, that sincerity with irony, a longing that nevertheless moves through the *Dreamsongs* quickly, nearly too fractured for eye or ear to manage, in and out of slapstick, through the public sound of bravado to the whispered aside and the clipped fragment that is as close as is presentable to weeping.

> Life, friends, is boring. We must not say so.
> After all, the sky flashes, the great sea yearns,
> we ourselves flash and yearn,
> and moreover my mother told me as a boy
> (repeatedly) "Ever to confess you're bored
> means you have no
>
> Inner Resources." I conclude now I have no
> inner resources, because I am heavy bored. . . .

And so the rebellious list of delicious boredoms goes on— "peoples," Berryman announces, and "literature, especially great literature" and "valiant art," and even, he says,

> . . . the tranquil hills, & gin, look like a drag
> and somehow a dog
> has taken itself & its tail considerably away
> to mountains or sea or sky, leaving
> behind: me, wag.

How the sound cascades down, the rich fulminating movement of the long sentence to the sad and comic fractured last phrase, is an audible play past reason into something more immediate, far more stricken. And such silence then; it deepens like a stain. I think of this, from Allen Ginsberg's interview years ago in the *Paris Review*: "I had the idea . . . that by the juxtaposition of one word against another . . . there'd be a gap between two words which the mind would fill with the sensation of existence. . . ." *Leaving / behind: me, wag.*

Between these two words, *me* and *wag*, we could be stranded a long time, our bemusement like the poet's, a kind of cool defense, all darkening. But more than words are juxtaposed: two moods—the serious and the comic, tragedy and a kind of deliberate goofy joy, a private agony under the public glad hand. Always in irony, this gap, and the mind fills or falls on that variant—silence in the talkative Berryman coming when we least expect it, our own lives for a moment mysterious, lost in it. In such a moment, we might be uncomfortably close to the whole point of making poems, this sweet and dangerous habit of mind I, at least, feel more and more uncertain about ever understanding.

There is a kind of birdsong that is particularly intriguing. The *quiet intense song*, Rosemary Jellis, the British ornithologist, calls it. Neither territorial nor sexual, it is sung by the bird only in solitude, head bowed, shivering its wings. One has to be very close to hear this song. Even so, in the dense leafy shade of summer one loses it. Sonargrams have shown it to be moving quickly but with great silences, hesitations between the very low and high notes. And all the time, this curious trembling of wing—though there is never flight—and the head neither thrown back or up, but drawn in, muffling the sound. Although it has been studied, some ornithologists deny it exists. And others? It means nothing, I heard one say. It has no purpose.

On Metaphor

Which is, at heart, a dream of sorts. Or veering off in half-dream, a surprise, this full creature life, and we stop, lean that much forward. The way the heart loses track for a second, skips and flutters back, and we're light-headed, just an instant of that light.

Evidence. Once, when I lived in Maine, a woman at the post office told me she had a letter for me, wait. She passed the pale envelope over the counter. No, not my name. Oh, she said, I'm sorry. You look just like her—are you sisters?—a red-haired woman who lives west of town? I laughed and told her I've never had a sister, though I have a neighbor who looks exactly like my brother. Oh, you have a brother then, she said, oddly relieved. On the steps outside, I realized my neighbor didn't look a thing like my brother; he just tells the same jokes.

Remote sensing. I think birds have it, knowing the distance they must fly precisely and absently, the map somewhere in their tiny brains, its shape the shape of their journey, and they land—I've seen sandhill cranes do this, October after October—in the same way in the same shattered cornfield, coming down weirdly, like huge broken kites, their voices terrible, the late sky dark with them. And why do I go each year to watch them, half delighted, half horrified? What shape in me matches this shape as I stand there with my bad binoculars, blurring them in and out, trying to focus?

Correspondence then, one thing so mysteriously *like* another, *this, just like this* says simile, says all metaphor, close and far. And isn't this what we watch in poems, the way things move and open out? This scene, from last spring: my friend and colleague, Margaret Rowe, who has thought a good deal on Auden, is talking with Adrienne Rich at a university reception before the lecture she, Rich, has come halfway across the country to give. It's all wine and small crackers but before long both women are wildly quoting Auden, this poem and that. The few of us standing close tilt our heads closer to hear each racing ahead, filling in words, phrases the other has forgotten. But they—all of us really—speak of Auden himself as well, Rich, of course, impatient with his sidestepping the truth of his sexual life in the poems, all that energy wasted in denial or avoidance. But what beautiful love poems all that avoidance made, Margaret is saying, the beloved cast as fish or bird or swan instead. I can see by Rich's face she thinks the method, if not the poems themselves, a smokescreen, pathetic or worse. And then those whose job it is to take her off to the lecture hall are suddenly here, ushering her out to the twilight street. But doesn't all art disguise, I think later, and isn't that the priceless thing, the careful eye on bird or fish and the inner eye elsewhere, metaphor in the poems letting loose its graceful flood of image and music? "That you, my swan," Auden wrote in 1936, "who have / all gifts that the swan / Impulsive nature gave / the majesty and pride / last night should add / your voluntary love." Remote sensing here too because the most important human things are private. Metaphor is defense of that fact, and in its secret way, release.

❦

The old Emily Dickinson line, perhaps, applies exactly to metaphor—to tell the truth but tell it slant. To edge sideways, like a crab, the eternal weight of ocean above, who can say how light or heavy. But we're stuck, not by equation but by unaccountable resemblance, Miss Marple, say, deciding somewhere in all those ageless Agatha Christie tangles that Mr. X surely must have done it because he's so much *like* Mr. Y from her old home village, equally tall and forgetful, staring with the same glass eye that doesn't move, ever. But we're caught there, in the gaze of that eye as Miss Marple chatters elsewhere in her smart, no-nonsense way. Because it's the full life buried in good metaphors that stops us. We get only a glimpse—the writer pointing *there* or *there*—then back so quickly because the real movement of the poem or the story is another way, a destination. But why this afterimage? Why this small persistence of vision, stubborn as the way light continues after the flashbulb fades, the neurons in the brain still at it, still blinding us?

I keep thinking, for instance, of this brief, spellbound passage in Brigit Kelly's long poem, "Three Cows and the Moon"—"And it was getting harder to see, /" she tells us, "But still the cows kept turning. There was the low / Cry of winter birds left back like dumb children kept behind in school." And though she rapidly goes on to the high bats and their "whistling and shuttling," then to the moon, I'm still back there, overcome by the dream of that digression—the birds somehow bringing up those children who too early know failure, their voices halfhearted, faint, the school yard vivid and years there—the small awkward kids we knew, the kids we were. *Sometimes our hearts are stone. Sometimes not,* she says some twelve lines earlier. Metaphor, that swift movement across time and space, is a place where stone does soften, where the willful forward movement toward resolution in the poem ceases—what thing *is* like this muffled call of far-off birds, what do we remember?—because the sound's too rich, too ancient to explain by explanation or by narrative, the reasonable *what happened next.*

The one simple thing about metaphor is that it moves us from one place to another, the word itself of restless parts, from buried Greek, *meta* meaning "over, across, behind" and *phoreo*—"to bring, bear, carry." In Athens these days, the biggest trucks of all, the moving vans, have *Metaphora* on their sides. You stand there and watch one get smaller and smaller before it turns the corner. ". . . like dumb children kept behind in school," Brigit Kelly writes, taking us back on that simile beyond the poem's visible world of field and pasture to the secret one, in memory. And returning then, in her poem, to the immediate cows and bats and moon, where are we really? Metaphor is a way of thinking in a poem but it's a way of slowing thought too, dreaming *off* on this seemingly rational thread of similarity. We control pace that way, perhaps scale; more important, we let the poem loose that way, tethered out on the thinnest line. Such sweetness, then, when that line nearly breaks.

It nearly breaks in Ellen Bryant Voigt's poem "The Last Class," which opens her third collection *The Lotus Flowers*. All along it's an ordinary bus trip spoken of, if long days and exhaustion are ordinary. The small events observed—a drunk bothering a woman across the Greyhound station, the wheezing heavy bus itself—are held eye level, no great fanfare. The view is transparent; we go through it to meet exactly what we recall of such a ride. It is relief then to feel the familiar scene lift as the poet goes inward, not in metaphor yet, but in self-questioning. "And ... who am I to teach the young?" she asks,

> having come so far from honest love of the world;
> I tried to recall how it felt
> to live without guilt; then I wrote down
> a few tentative lines about the drunk,
> because of an old compulsion to record,
> or sudden resolve not to be self-absorbed
> and full of dread—

A pause then, as the line ends abruptly on the dash, that split-second signal that Dickinson chose for its urgency or hopelessness or both, and then it's silence for the rest of the line, and into the next, not quite the vigil quiet of a stanza break but still that long intake of breath. "I wanted to salvage" she tells us,

> something from my life, to fix
> some truth beyond all change, the way
> photographers of war, miles from the front,
> lift print after print into the light
> each one further cropped and amplified,
> pruning whatever baffles or obscures,
> until the small figures are restored
> as young men sleeping.

Thinking of other ways this unsentimental meditation could have resolved itself without metaphor might be dangerous, or actively stupid. Still, the poem could have ended in a number of ways: more "comment upon" the nature of writing or sorrow for a high rhetorical finish, or a return to the ride itself, further careful observations—the snow-covered trees blurring or the woman bothered earlier sleeping now, one hand covering the other. But the depth of experience and sadness in the poem is rightly answered with metaphor, which is to say, only answered by a profound disappearance from this life to another. And so that blinding rush to the darkroom, the war photographer dutifully lifting print after print, just a job until by such tedious midnight effort, those miraculous "small figures" appear, those "young men sleeping."

What we witness here—what poetic energy is, at heart—is transformation. We literally time travel, recombine. All the scientists in their labs far under the street fooling with the very structure of matter hardly equal this. But what's lasting is the way we actually forget the bus station and the dread, forget the whole journey in the strange beauty of this other moment, the small sweet detail in the photograph coming into focus. Closure must open, must give us back the world somehow. Here the radiant thing is seen suddenly, in solitude, a brief safety amid all this danger. The way metaphor works is, in miniature, the way poetry itself works: release, compression, release. *It must change*, Wallace Stevens wrote, making his second arch and angelic requirement of poetry. In this case, we never return from the dream, the digression to the darkroom. We're too stunned by it.

❦

This movement out and in, the way metaphor so quickly alters even consumes the whole poem, to resist and get beyond its initial ambition—how do we learn that? Last Veterans Day, I listened while my neighbor, a grade school teacher, spoke of her students, her pride in them but mostly, this day, her annoyance: they can't concentrate on a single thing. For instance, Veterans Day, she says, and I'm holding up this flag. I'm trying to get them to talk about the flag, right? What it means, all the wars, all that. And they say, when did you get that flag? Someone gave it to me when my sister died, I tell them. And they say, you have a sister? Why did she die? What was wrong with her? Such questions, my neighbor says. And pretty soon I'm saying, look, she was sick a long time but we're here to think about Veterans Day. More questions, on and on. Her face is close to my face now. You see, she tells me, they can't learn about important things. She's working herself up now, some amusement left, but mostly anger. They can't hold a real thought and follow it.

But I'm stuck, like those kids, on this incredible scene— someone gives her a flag when her sister dies. Why would anyone do that? The children are right to be curious, I think. My neighbor isn't young; by all accounts she's good at her job. But I want to defend the kids. I bring up associative thinking, the connection of personal tragedies to public ones, how that's a form of reasoning too, how they're young and anyway death absorbs us in private ways long before the mind can hold a larger darkness like war, even a day frozen to remember all wars. She shakes her head. I ask them to discuss Veterans Day, not my life, she says. They just can't do it.

For a while that day, I thought about all those endless afternoons I spent in school at St. Bartholomew's, then St. Eugene's, so bored I didn't even see it as boredom, that drugged inwardness, that white noise. Where are we in such moments? I suppose it's like asking where we are when we sleep. Important years of this, really, an apprenticeship. It may well be the only real training we get for metaphor, for poetry. It's the secret life one makes that way, the imaginative life which goes as it goes, makes its own passionate shape. Eventually, I'm sure my neighbor did get her students back on track, to the level public verities of her subject. But for a moment they were elsewhere. Will *my* sister die? at least two of them must have still been thinking later, way into geography.

Robert Lowell somewhere calls a poem "a controlled hallucination" and surely metaphor, the way we leave things at hand for that sideways step, is itself within that hallucination, another smaller, more concentrated one, a poem within a poem, the best of them not ornament at all, not sugar. Poetic energy is outlaw energy—to define in some surprising, inevitable way. Make it new, Pound admonished, *ad nauseam*. But metaphor is hardly new, always part of the human imagination, greater or lesser affection for it, depending. It was Plato, of course, who had so famously thrown poets out of his ideal republic for coming at things with such lies. His student Aristotle was kinder, zeroing in on metaphor, at seeing real likenesses unobserved before, as exactly that thing which made a human being a poet in the first place. Back and forth, over centuries. Thomas Hobbes, Herbert Spencer, many scientists as well— Francis Bacon, Johannes Kepler among them. Even one of the shocking, William Harvey, writing his 1628 treatise on the circulation of the blood, used the conventional poetic excess of the day both to tame and enhance his idea. "This motion may be called circular in the way Aristotle says air and rain follow the circular motion of the stars," he wrote of the blood. "The moist earth warmed by the sun gives off vapors, which, rising, are condensed to fall again moistening the earth. By this means things grow. So also tempests and meteors originate by a circular approach and recession of the sun. Thus it happens in the body by the movement of the blood. . . ."

Sometimes when I see my neighbor, I still think of those children brightly dancing around singing out their terrible and goodwilled questions—a flag? Who gave you that flag? Why did your sister die? Curiosity must be largely what makes for metaphor: that, and the failure of the old ways to answer or explain. It may be we need the danger in it.

❦

This much about metaphor is always said: sameness, similarity, A=B as though such a neat, safe connection were possible. When possible is too possible, it hardens into cliché, goes sentimental because association is too close. It's mere definition then, too much already known, the sculptor Sylvia Shaw Judson once saying "Of course I made mistakes. Once I made such realistic owls on a bird bath that they frightened every bird for miles around." And in ordinary speech, we have that great *so what,* the old "red as a rose," "blue as the sky," "dark as night," as if any of this were news about these serious and eternal treasures, the rose and the sky, or night itself, never really commonplace. They describe perhaps, barely. They do not transform. Like Frost's famous straight walking stick that gave pleasure because of its crookedness, the best metaphor goes to its compulsory equation with some unwillingness, something left out to contradict or to charm. From Aristotle again, the first razor rule suggests this, both similarity and dissimilarity, the what-is-the-same floating uncannily, uneasily in the what-is-not.

When Laura Jensen says in "Kite," her remarkable poem about an old dime store, that after aisle upon aisle, in the progress from baby yarn and bibs to pencils and barrettes "a life has passed, a history, a generation," it is description, yes. We see these plain things but the transformation is swift, nearly tragic—sweet relics of a life now because the implied metaphor has abruptly changed the scale, altered what is at stake. Suddenly the view is aerial, immense, the dime store now a clicking time machine, the poem some time-lapsed movie, true but slightly ridiculous, like the kind that shows flowers growing a lifetime in thirty seconds. Then—"we're not looking / for some expensive kites now," the harried father tells his children who nevertheless "skip grandly around." Through them, we descend from metaphorical grandeur for a moment, restored to the human scale and comic possibilities of the scene. Later, of course, the breathless leap comes—the kite way above us now, this cheap thing rescued from its staged drama in the store window, made dangerous, mythic really, by flight. "Not kites in trees or kites like heroines / in wires," Jensen writes

> but the kite that was a speck,
> the opposite of fishing: to want nothing
> caught in anything but the pretty sky,
> to reel the color back down again
> beside you, a celebrity who tells
> what it is like in the altitude.

Like Ellen Voigt's surrender to the ending image of the war photographer who slowly makes his solitary discovery, Jensen stops here in the push and pull of this ordinary kite made extraordinary, free of wires, heroic and fine. And the whole process, too, is caught in glorious reverse—to fly a kite, "the opposite of fishing" she says, as if we could cast off to air and bring down color and sense. *As if.* But the metaphor carries a likeness in its longing and in the hand launching either the kite or the fishing line even as it doesn't equal—certainly water isn't air, and a kite never a thing really capable of memory or wonder. "All metaphor breaks down somewhere," Frost once blurted out, "That's the beauty of it." Like the beauty of light, say, which comes back to us as color only in that part of the wavelength that isn't absorbed by the object we stare at. It's the rejected part, the part not absorbed by the association that stays with us and *means* in metaphor, the part resisting, which will not be used, thank you, remaining singular, its own image, however briefly.

ꙮ

It's that stubbornness which might well be the secret praise in poems, a lyric Rorschach test to open things. All poems mime how we come to know human experience, even bad poems though what they probably mime is self-deception, the scale off, the pace all wrong. To sense dramatic shape in a poem is to feel metaphor working larger, the view expansive and minute at once. The meaning of the story, said Flannery O'Connor once, in defiance or exasperation, *is* the story. And so the poem goes underground, in abstraction, and out again to its concrete detail, all the intricacies of shape that mean as the body means sorrow or happiness—by gesture and pain, tension, repose.

There was a simple ride through the Indiana countryside I recall—this from a poem one of my undergraduate students, Jamie Crisman, wrote a couple of years ago—the road unusually hilly, past barns and houses, picturesque certainly, the sky blue behind the lilac bushes with their darker blue, the car's speed running all this splendor together. So far, all was fine, though the scene was predictable. But then abruptly—*around the next bend,* I want to say in the interest of suspense, but it wasn't that. Just there, suddenly in a stranger's pasture, were sheep, ten or twenty of them, all newly sheared, and this stunning detail: there was blood on the sheep. Even as the poet read this piece out loud, I could feel the thrill of that fact run through the class. It was spring in the poem and spring in that room. And the poem was right. In spring, sheep are cut from their wool thickened all winter and blood flows sometimes, dries there to a deeper color, smeared and kept intact by the dark red reddle used by farmers to mark the animals for shearing. An unexpected but inarguably reasonable thing to see on this drive through the country. *It must change,* Stevens said. And in that flash of blood, the road, the houses, the everything of this tidy world seemed changed. We fell through that piercing image, dropped down to the world under this one, darker now, more urgent. "Strangeness in beauty," Owen Barfield wrote in 1927, "arises from contact with a different kind of consciousness than our own."

But how do we find that consciousness locked as we insufferably are in our own? This is the metaphorical impulse at work, metaphor so often the occasion for the weird thing, the thing not-of-this-state-of-mind. Here the blood is a real image; one could see where the blade fell at an angle. But it works metaphorically to absorb the whole experience, the whole poem really—not the picturesque drive through the country, not the nice dinner party after all, but something else. And as swiftly as she left, the poet was back—to the same white farmhouses, gardens blurring by, the broken down mobile homes set back in woods but changed now by this flash from the underworld, blood left on the bald, vulnerable sheep who nevertheless wander the field as usual, lie down, sleep. Recently, in an interview with Peter Stitt, Stanley Kunitz said this:

> In the climactic action, the monumental door I knock on is the door of revelation. Many of my poems speak of a quest, the search for the transcendent, a movement from darkness into light, from the kingdom of the profane into the kingdom of

the sacred. As a rule, I don't feel I'm done with a poem until it passes from one realm of experience to another.

I think of those sheep exposed in the pasture, the wounds still visible from the road, how that single detail shatters the pretty surface—just an instant, a glance, but it is another realm, terrifying and in its way lovely. It should be called *metamorphosis*, this thing metaphor does, Stevens pointed out. Brief, this look, because perhaps that's all we can bear, because certain realizations come like this, unbidden, hard and elegant as glass. And Frost again—"Every poem is a new metaphor inside or it is nothing." Or maybe it's plainer than that, just genetic for the poet, whom Czeslaw Milosz defines in his poem "Reconciliation" as *one who constantly thinks of something else.*

ॐ

Or maybe it is even simpler—nothing about the observer but the world itself unfolding in random bits, Alice Munro saying once in interview that we live "in flashes," that "people don't develop and arrive somewhere at all." Metaphor must have been invented to get at those flashes, for its brave sideleaps from the safe main focus in the poem. Sometimes though, by dramatic juxtapositions, metaphor itself becomes the main focus, one focus after another in such a shifting. Frost said this surprising thing—"the most exciting movement in nature is not progress, advance, but expansion and contraction, the opening and shutting of the eye, the hand, the heart, the mind." Neuropsychologists tell us what is obvious about this, left over from our days as both prey and hunter, that any sort of movement is what the eye craves, that the head will turn every time toward it, this eye not simply an eye but one of the oldest parts of the brain.

Easy to get dizzy with certain writers then, Brazilian poet Adelia Prado for one. Virtually all her poems race and startle this way. In "Denouement," from her collection, *The Alphabet in the Park*, she begins with several lines of double take, her private vision of the ocean set against the public one of domestic duty. "They'd never guess I'm thinking of Tanzania," she almost stage-whispers to us, while her relatives happily show her their projects, "where the kitchen will be" and where they will dig out a garden. But the question that follows is a private one. "So what do I do with the coast?" she says of this internal world of large waters sealed within against the shared world of home and its ordinary business, so sensible.

One could stop a long time here and wonder what questions do in poems, the very sound and shape of them, their habit of signaling an end even as they suggest that something else is about to begin. What I love is the wait in them, the way a diver stands motionless, poised to do violence to the waters below. Questions hang there in this same quiet, their syntax pitched upward, thus miming the actual movement of the mind before its subject. But such stillness is a decoy. The movement's so swift we can't see it. "So what do I do with the coast?" Prado asks, idling before her leap to the next stanza, back to another "pretty afternoon," sitting among her uncles where she saw "the man with his fly open / the trellis angry with roses."

Juxtaposition, this habit of superimposing one image on another, is a more astonished way to make metaphor. Here the whole scene *enacts* what poetry always enacts, that great gulf between what is public and what is private. But how compressed the two worlds now, with the speaker sitting blankly "between uncles," seeing the open fly, the shock of what usually is hidden. Exactly because of the double take, we're launched into the roses so deeply that seeing them now is to see them moving and furious, not soothing, not at all the beauty we expect. To be transfixed here, however briefly, is to be transformed, the charge nearly electrical, shot from the niece through "the man with his fly open" to the roses no longer bound quaintly to their trellis. A glimpse, like the blood gleaming on the newly sheared sheep, of a world stranger and darker beneath this one. "No advance," said Frost, but "expansion and contraction, the opening and shutting of the eye, the head, the heart, the mind." Prado knows the power of her subject is not cheap, knows the sharper the flame, the quicker the hand says this, pulling away. Further juxtaposition expands it in quite another way. "Hours and hours we talked unconsciously in Portuguese, /" she recovers herself, purposeful and workaday, "as if it were the only language in the world."

From here, it's all invention inward: musing and most of all, longing, isolation deepened by the high opera of direct address to the moon and to the forests, to night itself whose sleep might save. And in the final brilliant sweep, we are back to the beginning equation. "Meanwhile everything is so small," she writes. "Compared to my heart's desire / the sea is a drop." Prado has said that metaphor is the guardian of reality. By its sidestep we move deeper into things as they are in the heart, and out there. "Who am I to organize the flight of a poem," she has said in defense of her wayward metaphorical turns that make shape. Not advance—where is there really to get to?—but expansion and contraction, the opening and shutting. So the whole poem is metaphor, how human consciousness shapes itself around what happens to it in the world, observing and refusing to observe. Even sentences do this, in miniature through syntax itself, the urgent direct address, her *oh moon, oh forests*, or *great cities*. This mimes too. Contemplation or ecstasy or both.

🦃

Even so, as much as metaphor opens to the world, perhaps first and last it is private equation, and half accident. Think what one does about Louise Bogan's hard and highly willed but vulnerable poems, the few that we have, the few that she didn't throw away in embarrassment or anger, there's this moment in her autobiographical prose collection, *Journey Around My Room*, which enters what Stevens calls the "vanishing point" of metaphor, past resemblance and nearing identity, self-definition coming without plan or wish. The site is her mother's hospital room, the poet almost eleven, and she's just seen the showy gift roses beside the bed, which she dislikes. But from the doorway, she notices something else, flowers that "gave me such a shock that I lost sight of the room for a moment." Flowers dark yellow and brown, simply arranged. But "a whole world," she remembered, in a moment, opened up: a world of . . . taste and know-ingness, that shot me forward . . . into an existence . . . con-cerning which, up to that instant of recognition, I had had no knowledge or idea . . . I saw the hands arranging the flowers and leaves, the water poured into the vase, the vase lifted to the shelf on which it stood: they were my hands. A garden from which such flowers came I could not visualize. I had never seen such a garden. But the impulse of pleasure that existed back of this arrangement—with its clear, rather severe emotional coloring—I knew. And I knew the flowers—their striped and mottled elegance . . . They were mine, as though I had invented them. The sudden marigolds. . . .

Not metaphor exactly, but certainly there is transformation in this long stare, a glimpse of the other realm Kunitz speaks of, a consciousness unimagined before the poet claims it. "They were my hands," Bogan writes with assurance, the fa-miliar thing abruptly focused—*what shape in me answers this shape?*—though her realization isn't really to claim but to re-lease, the way something remembered releases compassion or rage or joy into the air like a scent. In this we sense a first metaphor, giving names to things in the Eden we imagine the first of all gardens, such happy definition, this world without flaw, simply luck and lush circumstance. Note these words again: *I lost sight of the room for a moment.* And then the mind falls through marigolds, a whole "compressed story" there where the child lives bravely for a second but where the poet lives prophecy, a future beyond this room of worry and dread.

"Compressed story" was Howard Nemerov's way of speak-ing of metaphor. And especially in lyric poems, which move so completely on voice, on its authority and precision, metaphor can supply this sense of sequence, of story, lyrics being stub-born timeless creatures. In Louise Gluck's poem "Celestial Music," for instance, from her collection *Ararat*, we find a dream, and winter there, a friend who tells the speaker that "when you love the world, you hear celestial music: / look up. . . ." But the speaker finds nothing, "only clouds, snow, a white business in the trees / like brides leaping to a great height—" Though the conversation continues, in that initial intense and distracted shift out of the poem's immediate place—snow there in trees, white *as* brides leaping to a great height—we know instantly both the joy and doom of this classic moment, its history and future, *story* there, narrative. The brides' ecstasy is so high that it's blurred but we foresee the inevitable fall because of the metaphor, not public at all.

Metaphor by nature resists, it subverts; it's chameleon-like, changing as context changes, this thing Nemerov called "compressed story." It easily turns on us in more narrative pieces—compressed not-story-at-all. I think of Michael Ryan's poem "Switchblade" from his collection *God Hunger* which recalls a repeated scene from childhood, the father first cleaning then playing his three violins, the boy patient through all this, allowed finally a glimpse of his switchblade, steely veteran of so many fights in East St. Louis dance halls. And the boy's joy is part of the ritual because he anticipates, knowing already, even before it happens, the thrill of seeing and finally touching the knife with its "blade inside aching / to flash open." But metaphor works much earlier to set this mythic weight, those three violins taken out and placed side by side on the table. "They looked like children in coffins /" Ryan tells us, "three infant sisters whose hearts had stopped for no reason."

One could follow a compressed story here anyway, I suppose, inventing from this image the terrible mourning at the funeral, distraught parents and grandparents. One could, but we resist because the poem is filled with particulars already: how the table had been cleared from "the best meal," the polishing oil and rag used, and so on—the gathering of detail narrative demands and delights in. Now it's the mind wanting something else, some leak into another realm. Violin cases as coffins, violins themselves as so many small daughters whose hearts no longer work. These flashes take us out of the busy sequence to the stopped time one loves in the lyric, stopped here of course by death's literal weight, but stopped too because the moment itself is, the violins frozen by the image. And this effect is exactly *unlike* the frenzied moment in Louise Gluck's poem where the brides are leaping, and about to leap, her image born out of a great stillness in the poem where the speaker looks up, is stopped herself by what she sees, the racing "nothing" of cloud and snow. So metaphor answers, alters the very pace and ambition in poems. It's less a matter of design, I think, than of longing. We desire the other, whatever form that other takes.

❦

I read an interview recently, or part of one recalled by the Greek poet George Seferis in the introduction he wrote for Igor Stravinsky's *Poetics of Music*, a collection of lectures the composer gave in 1939 in the Charles Eliot Norton series at Harvard. In the lectures themselves, Stravinsky spoke simply of great mysteries, mysteries applying directly to poetry: that music is a succession of impulse and repose, that dissonance is a pure element of transition, that accidents are the only thing that really inspires. Seferis quotes from much later remarks too, an interview done in 1959 where Robert Craft asks Stravinsky about his habit of sleeping with the light on. The composer was straightforward. "I am able to sleep at night only when a ray of light enters my room from a closet or an adjoining chamber . . ." he said. "The light I still seek to be reminded of must have come . . . from the street lamp out my window on Krakow Canal . . . whatever it was, however . . . this umbilical cord of illumination still enables me at 78 to reenter the world of safety and enclosure I knew at 7 or 8."

Every night then, this ritual flooded the mind with images of another world, another realm, the ordinary light of New York or Boston or London transformed by this metaphorical rush to this old light of childhood, seeming, at least for the time it took to fall asleep, equally kind. I find all this haunting and even mythic in the plainest most aching way, the way mourning what is lost *almost* gives back, the way creation is so often re-creation. And the best of it done in solitude, on the slimmest thread of light.

But the other thing in this story of the great composer falling asleep is the process itself. Every night then the glow of the common lamp *became* this other light. The most curious thing about metaphor must be the way we can see it moving, see its intricate pulleys and gears working to take us out and elsewhere and sometimes back. Not just the surface of things, that pretty polished beauty we find in so many poems, but watching metaphor we witness the messy way the mind actually moves to make poems, the old back-of-the-tapestry or those awkward flying buttresses that hold up cathedrals.

When James Tate writes in "Entries," a piece from his early collection *Absences*, that "When I think no thing is like any other thing / I become speechless, cold. . . ." everything in the poem, probably rightly, stops. Still, the argument isn't finished. Tate closes in quite another way. "But when I say you are like / a swamp animal during an eclipse /" he tells us, "I am happy, full of wisdom, loved / by children and old men alike. / I am sorry if this confuses you," he adds. "During an eclipse, the swamp animal / acts as if day were night, drinking when he should be sleeping, etc. / This is why men stay up all night / writing to you."

In math years ago, I remember the teacher insisting that we *show our work*, not just the final equation but all the calculations, that awkward scribbled business it took to get there. Those mornings were long the way a year is long when you're nine or ten. I remember staring at the paper, perfectly senseless, truly hopeless, trying this small alleyway of numbers, trying that one, the whole complicated underruin of some ancient city dreamt or undiscovered. I remember most the weave and turning, all part of that reach to worlds I couldn't imagine but that might—almost—equal.

The Quiet House

The closest I've ever come to myth was that favorite game in college—we called it Earliest Memory, my friends sprawled out in someone's living room. *Moonlight on the bedroom floor* we'd say or *oh god, that fall down the steep back stairs.* . . . Still, I've always been puzzled: do we carry around these old images because we remember them or because they've been told to us over and over, a communal treasure? That river of milk, say, pouring down the long hallway in our tiny Chicago apartment one morning when I was four, and my mother, sitting down at the end of that white expanse, suddenly crying in the most hopeless way—did I see that? Or does it haunt me because my mother herself has held up this small scene, laughing: here's our funny, luckless, cherished life.

In fact, I don't have a very good memory; everyone tells me this. But poetry is a way of imaginative recall, bringing up detail, making it crucial. More, it's making shape, making these details mean in a way that nearly forgets the self—the poem as mere self-expression, *I hurt* or *I love*—to discover something out there, the first large shape, the house widening to street, to neighborhood, to world. How many women, then, in my mother's weeping that day, the hallway darkened and lit by shattered glass, the rushing wasted milk?

If memory is a matter of *place*, then my childhood gave me two. I was born in Chicago, spent thirteen years in its Catholic schools—as odd and eloquent and unreal as any education might be—moving from neighborhood to neighborhood three or four times, finally ending those years before college at its northwest edge where the cheap suburbs begin. The fixed point in all this was my father's parents—the Boruchs—my

Polish grandparents. I see them there in their old world house on Maplewood Avenue, the continual cabbage haze in the air, the rich rise and fall of a language my brother and I never understood, the Virgin Mary on the wall with her pierced heart, the silk fringed pillows—"Greetings from Manila"— their American-born sons sent back in 1944, so thrilled to be soldiers, to be away. "Ma, these are American children," I remember my father saying sadly, inscrutably to them once, one of the few times I heard him speak English in that house, standing in the doorway, hands in his pockets.

As counterpoint, I held my mother's world: small-town central Illinois, the place we went most of Christmas and Easter and much of the summer. The night train took us three hours south, the wheezing diesel clouds rising as the whole thing trembled, stood still, slowed by a signal light in the railroad tower—Tuscola not a stop on the regular line. I could make out my grandparents, the Taylors, there in their old coats to help us down the cold metal steps.

Where does imagination begin? My ordinary life was Chicago—school and afterschool and piano lessons and the noisy array of Boruch cousins, aunts, and uncles at the backyard barbecue. But Tuscola was the older, secret place, history a large part of its calm—gravestones with our family names chiseled in, four generations back of Taylors and Gills and Joneses. And my grandparents themselves—*old* grandparents, already in their seventies when I was born. Or perhaps, I've simply never gotten over the solemn joy of stepping down from that train into darkness, into that town, a square mile of houses and brick streets in the middle of prairie, and of course, into those arms waiting to lift my brother and me to the ground. From the track, I could see the beat-up taxi my grandparents had hired to take us to the house, its headlights dimmed, its radio soft; the driver had cracked his window open so the smoke from his cigar drifted out and up and disappeared. Meanwhile we couldn't stop talking, yelling really, my grandfather even then so deaf— news of school and the people they knew from visits north, our voices the only voices in the chill night air.

It's impossible—I fear, extinct—such a catalog of riches:

falling asleep later, the house of chiming ticking clocks, of pipe smoke and liniment, of line-dried sheets, stiff and rough from the wind. Outside wonders too: the train whistle again, which—from this distance—meant both routine and adventure, and in the morning, walks past the drugstore with its gory pictures of nineteenth-century operations set up in the window, or to Gus's for a fountain Coke or outside the old hotel where my grandfather stopped to talk to the ancient men leaning back in the metal chairs—the day warm enough—among them the one gassed in the First World War, Mr. Arthur, who couldn't speak, who just sat there blankly. *Mustard gas*, my mother had told me, and he had stared that way, she said, since the twenties when she was a kid.

Imagination might be tied up first, perhaps always, with mystery. I wanted, of course, to walk by the old men quickly, but my grandfather, who was, after all, one of them, stood and talked happily while I fidgeted on the sidewalk, my eye coming back to Mr. Arthur and whatever stony secret he kept locked inside. The slow shock of things: is this the beginning of poetry? I kept wishing for anything else—to be playing on the porch or in the battered side yard, to be talking endlessly in the kitchen with my grandmother about all my urgent nothings. Instead, it was my grandfather's usual exchange—the weather, corn prices, and as he claimed to be the town's only Democrat, certainly politics—all of it worth repeating a million times. But under their voices, Mr. Arthur loomed. Occasionally, he'd turn his head and look at me.

I need to be careful. It isn't some awful nostalgia that pulls me back to that look, nor is it even its historical weight. I don't think I ever woke out of nightmares because of him, and it was years before I learned the gruesome facts of trench warfare. No doubt the man dropped out of my head as soon as I could drag my grandfather off, taking his hand to cut across Sales Street to Main and straight home. It's more, perhaps, how Mr. Arthur's silence spoke, how his curious isolation mirrored some underside thing in me that felt sad and true and inevitable. That this town, so wonderfully picturesque with its band shell gazebo, its Andrew Carnegie Library, its bright heroic WPA mural in the post office, that such a place carried inside it another place, badly lit, seemingly senseless: this was news, memorable because that delicate, puzzling design repeated, made pattern.

The usual pattern of small towns, maybe: feuds, bad feeling as inherited as red hair, entire streets where my grandmother refused to walk for whatever reason. But against that, friends back to the 1880s, when my grandparents were children, one old lady so blind, she'd stoop and feel my face— slowly, lovingly—before saying hello. Various rituals of distress or pleasure; my brother and I were born to them, they were clear enough, meaning we largely accepted their mysteries. That is, until that mystery came home, and filled the quiet house.

It was something my grandmother told us herself one summer: when our Uncle Larry went to war—not Mr. Arthur's, but the Second World War—he went crazy. We were on the high sleeping porch off my grandfather's bedroom, a tiny screened-in place overlooking the backyard, smelling of dust, mothballs, and faintly, almost sweetly, of urine. My grandmother pointed to the trunk. Lawrence wrote a novel before he left, she told us, and god knows what was in it. But he locked it up, right there. Of course, he came back; we knew that much. He'd been in North Africa, the Italian campaign. But just raving by the time he got home, my grandmother was saying, shouting terrible things out the back door to Mrs. Helm, and then to the grocer, the preacher, even Tack Green, the undertaker—until he tore up the stairs and barricaded himself right here, on the porch. My brother and I sat there; I heard the neighbor's screen door bang, and a truck downshifting blocks away. My grandmother was slowing up now, but it was what came next that got me, how she found him later, standing in the cellar, feeding his novel, page by page, into the small flaming window of the coal furnace. It was dark down there, and all so private. She said nothing to him, turning back up the stairs, up and back into the bright kitchen.

Pattern is tension, the weave of opposites, imaginative engagement. Mr. Arthur's mute standstill among the arguing, wisecracking old men was one thing, but my uncle in the cellar, furious and without hope? I tried to think—still think—of this passionate, mad flash of him against the witty, startlingly urbane uncle we knew in Chicago who drove over from Oak Park with his cool, towering wife for an occasional Sunday afternoon. I think of the containment of that trunk, and the feverish denial of what was in it. As a kid, those afternoons of his visits, looking from the hallway, I kept eavesdropping as my uncle sipped his scotch, trying to figure some grave clue from the scene's slick surface.

I'll never get to the end of these mysteries—therefore I write poems, as Descartes surely meant to say. Of course Mr. Arthur but my uncle too, they're both dead now, and recently, since I live only ninety miles east of Tuscola these days, I drove back to that town, first finding where the hotel was—it burned to the ground in the mid-seventies—then parking on south Main in front of my grandparents' old house. It looked far shabbier, more desolate than I remembered, the green bamboo shades gone from the porch, the flowering spirea uprooted from the yard. I walked around back where the sleeping porch still hung off the second story like a thing dreamt up later, a last good idea.

It wasn't winter but spring, though I remembered one thing more about that trunk. My uncle's wool uniforms were in it, carefully folded khaki trousers and shirts, caps narrow as envelopes. The Christmas after we learned about the novel, my brother and I opened the trunk and put everything on, tying up the waists with string. Outside, the alley was one long frozen slick and we slid and fell and laughed, the pants rolled up but unrolling, the big sleeves flapping. I recall it perfectly, down to the most trivial detail. Still, I have this curious vision: I'm not playing at all, but alone in the house watching us play, looking down from the high back bedroom at these kids reeling and breathless, their clothes way too big for them.

References

Aristotle. *De Poetica*. Translated by Ingram Bywater. Oxford: The Clarendon Press, 1971.

Auden, W. H. *The Collected Shorter Poems*. New York: Random House, 1985.

Berryman, John. *77 Dreamsongs*. New York: Farrar, Straus and Giroux, 1970.

Bishop, Elizabeth. *The Complete Poems: 1927–1979*. New York: Farrar, Straus and Giroux, 1983.

Borges, Jorge Luis. *Labyrinths*. New York: New Directions, 1964.

Brown, Ashley. "An Interview with Elizabeth Bishop." *Shenandoah* 17:2 (1966).

Bache, William B. "On the Road to Innsbruck and Back." *The University Review—Kansas City* 34:3 (1968).

Barfield, Owen. *Poetic Diction*. London: Faber and Faber, 1928.

Bergonzi, Bernard. *Gerard Manley Hopkins*. New York: Macmillan, 1977.

Bogan, Louise. *Journey Around My Room*. Edited by Ruth Limmer. New York: Penguin Books, 1981.

———. *The Selected Letters of Louise Bogan*. Edited by Ruth Limmer. New York: Harcourt, Brace and Jovanovich, 1973.

Brooks, Cleanth, and Robert Penn Warren. *Understanding Poetry*. New York: Holt, Rinehart and Winston, 1950.

Compton, Elizabeth S. "Sylvia in Devon: 1962." *Sylvia Plath: The Woman and the Work*. Edited by E. Buttscher. London: P. Owen, 1979.

Cook, Reginald L. *Robert Frost: A Living Voice*. Amherst: University of Massachusetts Press, 1974.

Davenport, Guy. *The Geography of the Imagination*. San Francisco: North Point Press, 1981.

Dickinson, Emily. *The Letters of Emily Dickinson*. Edited by Thomas H. Johnson. Cambridge: Harvard University Press, 1958.

————. *The Complete Poems of Emily Dickinson*. Edited by Thomas H. Johnson. Boston: Little, Brown, 1955.

Edson, Russell. "The Prose Poem in America." *Parnassus* 5:1 (1976).

Eliot, T. S. *The Complete Poems and Prose of T. S. Eliot*. New York: Harcourt, Brace, 1952.

Fargus, Frederick. *Called Back*. New York: H. Holt and Co., 1884.

Francis, Robert. *Collected Poems 1936–1976*. Amherst: University of Massachusetts Press, 1976.

Frank, Elizabeth. *Louise Bogan*. New York: Knopf, 1985.

Frost, Robert. *The Poetry of Robert Frost*. Edited by Edward Conney Lathem. New York: Holt, Rinehart and Winston, 1969.

————. *The Selected Prose of Robert Frost*. New York: Holt, Rinehart and Winston, 1956.

Ginsberg, Allen. "The Art of Poetry." *The Paris Review* 37:10 (1966).

Gluck, Louise. *Ararat*. New York: Ecco, 1990.

Graham, Jorie. *The End of Beauty*. New York: Ecco, 1987.

Gross, Harvey. *Sound and Form in Modern Poetry*. Ann Arbor: University of Michigan Press, 1968.

Hall, Donald. "Goatfoot, Milktongue, Twinbird." *Claims for Poetry*. Edited by Donald Hall. Ann Arbor: University of Michigan Press, 1982.

Hamilton, David. "An Interview with Donald Hall." *The Iowa Review* 15:1 (1985).

Hancock, Geoff. "An Interview with Alice Munro." *Canadian Fiction Magazine* 43 (1982).

Harvey, William. *Anatomical Studies on the Motion of the Heart and Blood*. Translated by C. Leake. Springfield, Ill.: C. C. Thomas, 1978.

Hass, Robert. From a talk given on trends in contemporary poetry. Wabash College, Crawfordsville, Ind. March, 1990.

————. *Twentieth Century Places: Prose on Poetry*. New York: Ecco, 1984.

Hawking, Steven W. *A Brief History of Time*. New York: Bantam, 1988.

Hayden, Robert. *The Collected Poems of Robert Hayden*. Edited by Frederick Glaysher. New York: Liveright, 1985.

Heaney, Seamus. *The Government of the Tongue: Selected Prose 1978–1987*. New York: Farrar, Straus and Giroux, 1989.

Hoffman, Malvina. *Sculpture Inside and Out*. New York: Norton, 1939.

————. *Yesterday is Tomorrow*. New York: Crown, 1965.

Hopkins, Gerald Manley. *Further Letters of Gerard Manley Hopkins*. Edited by C. C. Abbot. London: Oxford University Press, 1958.

————. *The Letters of Gerard Manley Hopkins to Robert Bridges*. Edited by C. C. Abbot. London: Oxford University Press, 1955.

————. *The Notebooks and Papers of Gerard Manley Hopkins*. Edited by

Humphrey House and Graham Storey. London: Oxford University Press, 1959.

———. *The Poems and Prose of Gerard Manley Hopkins*. Edited by W. H. Gardner. New York: Penguin Books, 1986.

Jarrell, Randall. *Poetry and the Age*. New York: Farrar, Straus and Giroux, 1953.

Jellis, Rosemary. *Bird Sounds and their Meaning*. Ithaca, N.Y.: Cornell University, 1984.

Jensen, Laura. *Memory*. Port Townsend, Wash.: Dragon Gate, 1982.

Judson, Sylvia Shaw. *For Gardens and Other Places: The Sculpture of Sylvia Shaw Judson*. Chicago: Henry Regnery Co., 1967.

Kees, Weldon. *The Collected Poems of Weldon Kees*. Edited by Donald Justice. Lincoln: University of Nebraska Press, 1975.

Keller, Lynn. "Words Worth a Thousand Postcards: The Bishop/Moore Correspondence." *American Literature* 55:3 (1983).

Kelly, Brigit Pegeen. "Three Cows and the Moon." *The New England Review* 15:4 (1993).

Langstroth, Lorenzo and C. P. Dadant. *The Hive and the Honey Bee*. Edited by Dadant and Sons. Hamilton, Ill.: Dadant and Sons, 1978.

Levertov, Denise. "On the Function of the Line." *Claims for Poetry*. Edited by Donald Hall. Ann Arbor: University of Michigan Press, 1982.

Levine, Philip. *A Walk with Tom Jefferson*. New York: Knopf, 1988.

Lopez, Barry. "Interview: Charles Simic." *Skywriting* 1:2 (1972).

Loyola, Ignatius. *The Spiritual Exercises of Ignatius Loyola*. Translated by Anthony Mottola. New York: Doubleday, 1964.

Macaulay, Rose. *The Pleasure of Ruins*. London: Weidenfeld and Nicolson, 1953.

Manley, R. *Beekeeping in Britain*. London: Faber and Faber, 1948.

Marianne Moore Issue. *Quarterly Review of Literature* 4:2 (1948).

Merwin, W. S. *The Carrier of Ladders*. New York: Athenaeum, 1973.

Milosz, Czeslaw. *Bells in Winter*. New York: Ecco, 1978.

———. *Province*. New York: Ecco, 1991.

Moore, Marianne. Artwork, XIII, Box 1 and 3. Marianne Moore Collection of the Rosenbach Museum and Library, Philadelphia, Pa.

Moore, Marianne. *The Complete Poems of Marianne Moore*. New York: Viking, 1967.

———. *The Complete Prose of Marianne Moore*. Edited by Patricia Willis. New York: Viking, 1986.

Nemerov, Howard. *New and Selected Essays*. Carbondale: Southern Illinois University Press, 1985.

O'Connor, Flannery. *Mystery and Manners*. New York: Farrar, Straus and Giroux, 1969.

Olson, Charles. *Human Universe*. New York: Grove Press, 1967.

Orr, Gregory. *New and Selected Poems*. Middletown, Conn.: Wesleyan University Press, 1988.

Orr, Peter. "An Interview with Sylvia Plath." Recording made for the British Broadcasting Corporation, October 1962. Issued from Credo Records, Cambridge, Mass. as "Plath Reads Plath," 1975, made under the auspices of the British Council and the Woodberry Poetry Room, Harvard College Library.

Oppen, George. *Of Being Numerous*. New York: New Directions, 1968.

―――. "Selections from George Oppen's Daybook." *The Iowa Review* 18:3 (1988).

―――. *This is Which*. New York: New Directions, 1968.

Patterson, Rebecca. *The Riddle of Emily Dickinson*. Boston: Houghton Mifflin, 1951.

Perloff, Marjorie. "The Two Ariels: The (Re)Making of the Sylvia Plath Canon." *American Poetry Review* November/December, 1984.

Plath, Otto. *Bumblebees and their Ways*. New York: Macmillan, 1934.

Plath, Sylvia. Drafts of the bee sequence from the *Ariel* Collection of the Manuscript Collection of Sylvia Plath, William Allan Neilson Library, Smith College, Northampton, Mass.

―――. *Johnny Panic and the Bible of Dreams: Short Stories, Prose and Diary Excerpts*. Edited by Ted Hughes. New York: Harper and Row, 1977.

―――. *The Journal of Sylvia Plath*. Edited by Ted Hughes and Frances McCullough. New York: Dial, 1982.

―――. *Letters Home*. Edited by Aurelia Schober Plath. London: Faber and Faber, 1975.

―――. *The Collected Poems of Sylvia Plath*. Edited by Ted Hughes. New York: Harper and Row, 1981.

Prado, Adelia. *The Alphabet in the Park*. Translated by Ellen Watson. Middletown, Conn.: Wesleyan University Press, 1990.

Rich, Adrienne. *On Lies, Secrets and Silence*. New York: Norton, 1979.

Rilke, Rainer Maria. *The Duino Elegies*. Translated by Stephen Garmey and Jay Wilson. New York: Harper and Row, 1977.

Rodin, Auguste. *On Art and Artists*. New York: Philosophical Library, 1957.

Roethke, Theodore. *The Collected Poems of Theodore Roethke*. Garden City, N.Y.: Doubleday, 1966.

Ruskin, John. *The Elements of Drawing*. New York: Wiley, 1876.

Ryan, Michael. *God Hunger*. New York: Viking, 1989.

Seager, Allan. *The Glass House*. New York: McGraw Hill, 1968.

Schulman, Grace. "Conversation with Marianne Moore." *Quarterly Review of Literature* 19:1–2 (1974).

————. "Sylvia Plath and Yaddo." *Ariel Ascending: Writings about Sylvia Plath*. Edited by P. Alexander. New York: Harper and Row, 1985.

Sergeant, Elizabeth Shepley. *Robert Frost: the Trial by Existence*. New York: Holt, Rinehart and Winston, 1960.

Sewall, Richard. *The Life of Emily Dickinson*. New York: Farrar, Straus and Giroux, 1974.

Sexton, Anne. *A Self-Portrait in Letters*. Edited by Linda Gray Sexton and Lois Amers. Boston: Houghton Mifflin, 1977.

Simic, Charles. *Classic Ballroom Dances*. New York: Braziller, 1980.

Simmel, George. *Essays on Sociology, Philosophy and Aesthetics*. Edited by Kurt H. Wolff. New York: Harper and Row, 1959.

Stapleton, Laurence. *Marianne Moore: The Poet's Advance*. Princeton, N. J.: Princeton University Press, 1978.

Stevens, Wallace. *The Letters of Wallace Stevens*. Edited by Holly Stevens. New York: Knopf, 1966.

————. *The Necessary Angel*. New York: Knopf, 1951.

————. *Opus Posthumous*. New York: Knopf, 1957.

————. *The Collected Poems of Wallace Stevens*. New York: Random House, 1982.

Stitt, Peter. "An Interview with Stanley Kunitz." *The Gettysburg Review* 5:1 (1992).

Storey, Graham. *A Preface to Hopkins*. London: Longman, 1981.

Stravinsky, Igor. *The Poetics of Music*. Cambridge: Harvard University Press, 1942.

Festschrift for Marianne Moore's Seventy-Seventh Birthday. Edited by Tambimuttu. New York: Tambimuttu and Mass, 1964.

Tate, James. *Absences*. Boston: Little, Brown, 1972.

Thompson, Lawrance and R. H. Winnick. *Robert Frost: The Later Years*. New York: Holt, Rinehart and Winston, 1976.

Vendler, Helen. "Who is Sylvia?" *New Republic* November 6, 1989.

Voigt, Ellen Bryant. *The Lotus Flowers*. New York: Norton, 1987.

Wagner, Linda W. *Sylvia Plath, the Critical Heritage*. Edited by Linda W. Wagner. London: Routledge, 1988.

Williams, William Carlos. *Selected Essays*. New York: Random House, 1954.

————. *The Selected Poems of William Carlos Williams*. New York: New Directions, 1969 and 1985.

Wolff, Cynthia Griffin. *Emily Dickinson*. New York: Knopf, 1986.

UNDER DISCUSSION
Donald Hall, General Editor

Volumes in the Under Discussion series collect reviews and essays about individual poets. The series is concerned with contemporary American and English poets about whom the consensus has not yet been formed and the final vote has not been taken. Titles in the series include:

Elizabeth Bishop and Her Art
edited by Lloyd Schwartz and Sybil P. Estess
Richard Wilbur's Creation
edited and with an Introduction by Wendy Salinger
Reading Adrienne Rich
edited by Jane Roberta Cooper
On the Poetry of Allen Ginsberg
edited by Lewis Hyde
Robert Creeley's Life and Work
edited by John Wilson
On the Poetry of Galway Kinnell
edited by Howard Nelson
On Louis Simpson
edited by Hank Lazer
Anne Sexton
edited by Steven E. Colburn
James Wright
edited by Peter Stitt and Frank Graziano
Frank O'Hara
edited by Jim Elledge
On the Poetry of Philip Levine
edited by Christopher Buckley
The Poetry of W. D. Snodgrass
edited by Stephen Haven
Denise Levertov
edited by Albert Gelpi
On William Stafford
edited by Tom Andrews

Please write for further information on available editions and current prices.

Ann Arbor   University of Michigan Press